Cambridge Elements

Elements in Soviet and Post-Soviet History
edited by
Mark Edele
University of Melbourne
Rebecca Friedman
Florida International University

THE FATE OF THE SOVIET BLOC'S MILITARY ALLIANCE

Reform, Adaptation, and Collapse of the Warsaw Pact, 1985–1991

Mark Kramer
Harvard University

Shaftesbury Road, Cambridge CB2 8EA, United Kingdom

One Liberty Plaza, 20th Floor, New York, NY 10006, USA

477 Williamstown Road, Port Melbourne, VIC 3207, Australia

314–321, 3rd Floor, Plot 3, Splendor Forum, Jasola District Centre, New Delhi – 110025, India

103 Penang Road, #05–06/07, Visioncrest Commercial, Singapore 238467

Cambridge University Press is part of Cambridge University Press & Assessment, a department of the University of Cambridge.

We share the University's mission to contribute to society through the pursuit of education, learning and research at the highest international levels of excellence.

www.cambridge.org
Information on this title: www.cambridge.org/9781009557207

DOI: 10.1017/9781009557160

© Mark Kramer 2025

This publication is in copyright. Subject to statutory exception and to the provisions of relevant collective licensing agreements, no reproduction of any part may take place without the written permission of Cambridge University Press & Assessment.

When citing this work, please include a reference to the DOI 10.1017/9781009557160

First published 2025

A catalogue record for this publication is available from the British Library

ISBN 978-1-009-55720-7 Hardback
ISBN 978-1-009-55715-3 Paperback
ISSN 2753-5290 (online)
ISSN 2753-5282 (print)

Cambridge University Press & Assessment has no responsibility for the persistence or accuracy of URLs for external or third-party internet websites referred to in this publication and does not guarantee that any content on such websites is, or will remain, accurate or appropriate.

The Fate of the Soviet Bloc's Military Alliance

Reform, Adaptation, and Collapse of the Warsaw Pact, 1985–1991

Elements in Soviet and Post-Soviet History

DOI: 10.1017/9781009557160
First published online: January 2025

Mark Kramer
Harvard University
Author for correspondence: Mark Kramer, mkramer@fas.harvard.edu

Abstract: When Mikhail Gorbachev became the leader of the Soviet Union in 1985, the Warsaw Pact was a robust military alliance. It was capable of waging a large-scale war in Europe and was an instrument of Soviet hegemony in Eastern Europe, keeping orthodox Communist regimes in power. The alliance over the years had also become an effective mechanism of political coordination and consultation. In April 1985, the Warsaw Pact leaders met in Warsaw and renewed the Pact for another thirty years. Yet only six years later, the alliance was disbanded, having been rendered obsolete by the political transformation of Eastern Europe in 1989–1990. This monograph recounts what happened to the Warsaw Pact during its final years and explains why the organization ceased to exist in 1991.

This Element also has a video abstract: http://www.cambridge.org/ESPH-Kramer

Keywords: Soviet Union, Warsaw Pact, military alliances, Communist states, Mikhail Gorbachev, East-Central Europe

© Mark Kramer 2025

ISBNs: 9781009557207 (HB), 9781009557153 (PB), 9781009557160 (OC)
ISSNs: 2753-5290 (online), 2753-5282 (print)

Contents

Introduction	1
Early Signs of Continuity and Change	12
The Warsaw Pact's New Military Doctrine	22
Restructuring and Reductions of Forces	28
Reorientation of Soviet Policy	34
The Secret Reinterpretation of Soviet Obligations under the Warsaw Pact	36
The Dissolution of East European Communism	43
Disbandment of the Warsaw Pact	46
Conclusions	53
Select Bibliography	55

Introduction

In the closing months of World War II and the latter half of the 1940s, the Soviet Union oversaw the establishment of Communist regimes throughout Central and Eastern Europe. Over the next four decades, those regimes together with the USSR constituted what was informally known as the Soviet bloc. To help ensure the maintenance of Communist rule in East-Central Europe, the Soviet Union set up a military alliance system with the other countries in the bloc, initially through an interlocking series of bilateral defense agreements. At a meeting in Warsaw on May 14, 1955, the USSR and most of the East European states signed documents creating a formal multilateral alliance.[1] This new allied structure, known as the Warsaw Treaty Organization (or Warsaw Pact, for short), started out primarily as a buffer zone for the USSR rather than a full-fledged military organization.

The formation of the Warsaw Pact came a day before the Soviet Union joined the United States, Great Britain, France, and Austria in signing the Austrian State Treaty, which, among other things, provided for the withdrawal of all Soviet and Western occupation forces from Austria.[2] Until May 1955, the ostensible justification for Soviet military deployments in both Hungary and Romania had been that they were needed to preserve logistical and communications links with Soviet troops in Austria. The signing of the Austrian State Treaty would have eliminated the purported justification for the continued deployment of Soviet miliary units in Hungary and Romania, but the establishment of the multilateral Warsaw Pact the previous day provided a fresh rationale for keeping Soviet troops in those two countries even after all Soviet troops pulled out of Austria.

Although the signing of the Warsaw Pact was intended mainly as a symbolic counter to the admission of West Germany into the North Atlantic Treaty Organization (NATO), the legitimacy it conferred on the Soviet troop presence in allied countries was part of a larger Soviet effort under Nikita Khrushchev to codify the basic political and military structures of Soviet–East European relations. The status-of-forces agreements the Soviet government concluded with Poland (1956), Hungary (1957), East Germany (1957), Romania (1957), and Czechoslovakia

---

[1] "Podpisanie dogovora o druzhbe, sotrudnichestve i vzaimnoi pomoshchi," *Pravda* (Moscow), May 15, 1955, p. 1, and the text of the treaty on p. 2. The member-states, in addition to the Soviet Union, were Albania, Bulgaria, Czechoslovakia, East Germany, Hungary, Poland, and Romania. Albania withdrew from the Pact in 1968.
[2] Gerald Stourzh and Wolfgang Mueller, *A Cold War over Austria: The Struggle for the State Treaty, Neutrality, and the End of East-West Occupation, 1945–1955* (Lanham, MD: Lexington Books, 2018); Arnold Suppan, Gerald Stourzh, and Wolfgang Mueller, eds., *Der österreichische Staatsvertrag* (Vienna: Böhlau, 2005); and Mark Kramer, "The USSR and Cold War Neutrality and Nonalignment in Europe," in Mark Kramer, Aryo Makko, and Peter Ruggenthaler, eds., *The Soviet Union and Cold War Neutrality and Nonalignment in Europe* (Lanham, MD: Rowman & Littlefield, 2021), pp. 533–565.

(1968), which devolved a large share of the stationing costs to the host countries, were bilateral in nature, but they bolstered the Warsaw Pact insofar as they gave the Soviet Union a reliable means of ensuring the indefinite continuation of the "temporary" presence of its ground and air forces in East-Central Europe.[3]

During the first several years after the Warsaw Pact was formed, the military role of the alliance was relatively meager, limited mainly to the integration of strategic air defense forces under Soviet command. When a severe crisis erupted in Hungary in the autumn of 1956, the Romanian, Bulgarian, and Czechoslovak authorities expressed willingness (even eagerness) to have their own troops take part alongside Soviet forces in what would have been a Warsaw Pact operation to quell the revolutionary unrest in Hungary, but the Soviet Union decided not to use the Pact and instead relied exclusively on its own army to crush the rebellion.[4] Although many of the Soviet troops entered Hungary from the territory of another Warsaw Pact member-state, Romania, this was undertaken via the USSR's bilateral defense agreement with Romania, rather than under the auspices of the Warsaw Pact.[5] Not until the early 1960s, when Soviet and East European troops initiated a series of joint military exercises connected with the Berlin crisis and Soviet leaders started pressuring the East European countries to expand and modernize their armies, did the alliance begin to take on greater significance for intra-bloc contingencies as well as external defense.

In 1968 the commander-in-chief of the Warsaw Pact's joint armed forces, Marshal Ivan Yakubovskii, played a key role during the Soviet-Czechoslovak crisis, particularly in organizing military exercises that were designed to intimidate the Czechoslovak authorities and population. Yakubovskii was originally slated to command the Soviet and East European military contingents that invaded Czechoslovakia in August 1968, but at the last minute he had to relinquish that assignment because Soviet Defense Minister Andrei Grechko, who had long disliked Yakubovskii, did not want him to get credit for overseeing the joint operation.[6] On August 17, a few days before the invasion of Czechoslovakia began, Grechko persuaded the leaders of the Communist Party of the Soviet Union (CPSU) to transfer control of allied forces from Yakubovskii and the Main Staff of

---

[3] For an astute appraisal, see U.S. Central Intelligence (CIA), "The Warsaw Pact: Its Role in Soviet Bloc Affairs from Its Origin to the Present Day," Intelligence Analytical Report, May 6, 1966, released September 2002, available in CIA, Electronic Reading Room (ERR), <www.cia.gov/library/readingroom/home>.

[4] Mark Kramer, "The Soviet Union and the 1956 Crises in Hungary and Poland: Reassessments and New Findings," *Journal of Contemporary History*, Vol. 33, No. 2 (April 1998), pp. 163–214.

[5] See Document No. 49 in Ioan Scurtu, ed., *România: Retragerea trupelor sovietice. 1958* (Bucharest: Didactică și Pedagogică, 1996), pp. 247–249.

[6] Mark Kramer, "The Kremlin, the Prague Spring, and the Brezhnev Doctrine," in Vladimir Tismaneanu, ed., *Promises of 1968: Crisis, Illusion, and Utopia* (Budapest: Central European University Press, 2011), pp. 251–252.

the Warsaw Pact to the Soviet High Command, a move that necessitated extensive last-minute reworking of combat directives and plans for an operation that was ultimately placed under the supervision of Army-General Ivan Pavlovskii, the commander-in-chief of Soviet Ground Forces.

This abrupt change of command authority was highly unusual, but it did not adumbrate a downgrading of the Warsaw Pact per se. Even though supreme control of the operation was transferred at the last moment from the allied Joint Command to the Soviet High Command, the Warsaw Pact's role in the crisis up to that point had been salient throughout and remained so afterward.[7] Brezhnev was determined to give the invasion a multilateral appearance (unlike the unilateral action in Hungary in 1956), and he obtained the cooperation of four other Warsaw Pact countries – East Germany, Poland, Bulgaria, and Hungary – to intervene with the Soviet Union against their ally, Czechoslovakia (though in the case of East Germany only a liaison unit took part after the Polish leader Władysław Gomułka and Czechoslovak hardliners warned Brezhnev that the entry of East German combat troops onto Czechoslovak territory would trigger a political backlash).[8]

The function that the Warsaw Pact performed in 1968 as a defender of "socialist gains" in Czechoslovakia was the touchstone for subsequent crises in Eastern Europe. In the wake of the 1968 invasion, Soviet officials and commentators enunciated what became known in the West as the Brezhnev Doctrine (named after the then leader of the USSR, Leonid Brezhnev). This "doctrine" linked the fate of each Warsaw Pact country with the fate of all others, stipulated that every member of the Pact must abide by the norms of Marxism-Leninism as interpreted in Moscow, and rejected "abstract sovereignty" in favor of the "laws of class struggle."[9] The Brezhnev Doctrine thus laid out even stricter "rules of the game" than in the past for the Soviet bloc:

> Without question, the peoples of the socialist countries and the Communist parties have and must have freedom to determine their country's path of development. Any decision they make, however, must not be inimical either

---

[7] For more on this, see ibid., pp. 358–360.
[8] See Gomulka's secret speech on August 29, 1968 at a plenum of the Central Committee of the Polish United Workers' Party, reproduced in "Gomułka o inwazji na Czechoslowacje w sierpniu '68: Mysmy ich zaskoczyli akcja wojskowa," *Polityka* (Warsaw), No. 35 (August 29, 1992), p. 13. The most authoritative analyses of the role of the East German Nationale Volksarmee (NVA) during the invasion have been produced by Rüdiger Wenzke, including his *Prager Frühling – Prager Herbst: Zur Intervention der Warschauer-Pakt-Streitkräfte in der ČSSR 1968, Fakten und Zusammenhange* (Berlin: Dunckere Humblot, 1990); and *Die NVA und der Prager Frühling 1968: Die Rolle Ulbrichts under der DDR-Streitkräfte bei der Niederschlagung der tschechoslowakischen Reformbewegung* (Berlin: Links Verlag, 1995).
[9] "Zashchita sotsializma – vysshii internatsional'nyi dolg," *Pravda* (Moscow), August 22, 1968, pp. 2–3; and S. Kovalev, "Suverenitet i internatsional'nye obyazannosti sotsialisticheskikh stran," *Pravda* (Moscow), September 26, 1968, p. 4.

to socialism in their own country or to the fundamental interests of the other socialist countries ... A socialist state that is in a system of other states composing the socialist commonwealth cannot be free of the common interests of that commonwealth. The sovereignty of individual socialist countries cannot be set against the interests of world socialism and the world revolutionary movement.... Each Communist party is free to apply the principles of Marxism-Leninism and socialism in its own country, but it is not free to deviate from these principles if it is to remain a Communist party.... The weakening of any of the links in the world system of socialism directly affects all the socialist countries, and they cannot look indifferently upon this.[10]

The Warsaw Pact's founding charter had stipulated that the organization was supposed to be "open to all states ... irrespective of their social and political systems," but the Brezhnev Doctrine made clear that the members of the Pact would have to conform with the "common natural laws of socialist development, deviation from which could lead to a deviation from socialism as such." The Soviet Union reserved for itself the right to determine when "deviations" from the "common natural laws of socialist development" exceeded permissible bounds, and Soviet leaders claimed that Warsaw Pact members had a "sacred duty" to intervene when necessary to "protect socialist gains."[11]

After the enunciation of the Brezhnev Doctrine, Soviet officials and military commanders repeatedly emphasized that the use of force to keep orthodox Communist regimes in power was one of the chief military missions of the Warsaw Pact.[12] That function came to the fore in 1980–1981, when Marshal Viktor Kulikov, who had succeeded Yakubovskii in 1976 as commander-in-chief of the Pact's joint armed forces, played a crucial political as well as military role vis-à-vis Poland during the prolonged crisis that followed the emergence of the independent Solidarity labor movement in the summer of 1980.[13] In late August 1980, the CPSU Politburo authorized the mobilization of 100,000 Soviet

---

[10] Kovalev, "Suverenitet i internatsional'nye obyazannosti," p. 4.

[11] See the discussion in Kramer, "The Kremlin, the Prague Spring, and the Brezhnev Doctrine," pp. 362–370.

[12] See, for example, Army-General S. M. Shtemenko, "Bratstvo rozhdennoe v boyu," *Za rubezhom* (Moscow), No. 19 (May 1976), p. 7.

[13] Mark Kramer, "The Soviet Union, the Warsaw Pact, and the Polish Crisis of 1980–1981," in Lee Trepanier, Spasimir Domaradzki, and Jaclyn Stanke, eds., *The Solidarity Movement and Perspectives on the Last Decade of the Cold War* (Kraków: Oficyna Wydawoicza, 2010), pp. 27–67; Mark Kramer, "Die Sowjetunion, der Warschauer Pakt und blockinterne Krisen während der Brežnev-Ära," in Torsten Diedrich, Winfried Heinemann, and Christian Ostermann, eds., *Der Warschauer Pakt: Von der Gründung bis zum Zusammenbruch 1955–1991* (Berlin: Ch. Links, 2008), pp. 273–337; Mark Kramer, *Soviet Deliberations during the Polish Crisis, 1980–1981*, CWIHP Special Working Paper No. 1 (Washington, DC: Cold War International History Project, 1999); Mark Kramer, *The Kukliński Files and the Polish Crisis of 1980–1981: An Analysis of the Newly Released Documents on Ryszard Kukliński*, CWIHP Working Paper No. 59 (Washington, DC: Cold War International History Project, March 2009); Mark Kramer,

combat troops "in case military assistance is provided to Poland" by the Warsaw Pact. Kulikov oversaw numerous bilateral and multilateral military exercises in and around Poland, and he traveled to Warsaw many times on behalf of the CPSU Politburo and the USSR Defense Council to push for and facilitate the introduction of martial law by Polish forces.

Detailed plans for Soviet/Warsaw Pact military intervention in Poland were drafted, and in December 1980 and April 1981 large numbers of Soviet, East German, and Czechoslovak soldiers were mobilized for joint military action in Poland, though ultimately they were not sent in. A similar scenario could have materialized in December 1981 if the Polish Communist regime's operation to impose martial law had gone awry, causing civil war to erupt in Poland and endangering Soviet troops there.[14] But, as it turned out, the swift and successful introduction of martial law in Poland in December 1981 without the involvement of troops from other Warsaw Pact countries enabled Soviet leaders to avoid having to decide whether to move ahead with an invasion.

The Warsaw Pact's role in upholding orthodox Communist regimes in Eastern Europe against serious internal threats was reinforced by the alliance's military strategy, which in effect preserved a Soviet capability to intervene in other member-states. Warsaw Pact strategy was essentially identical to Soviet strategy for Europe in its emphasis on a blitzkrieg-style assault by combined Soviet and East European forces against NATO positions in Western Europe.[15] To support this strategy, the military establishments in Eastern Europe (other than Romania from the mid-1960s on) geared most of their training, tactics, and military planning toward offensive operations and devoted little time to defensive arrangements that would have impeded Soviet intervention in their own countries. Even the unique system of National Territorial Defense (*Obrona terytorium kraju*) in Poland, though defensive in nature, was designed entirely to protect against nuclear air attacks from the West. By inducing the East European states to concentrate exclusively on perceived threats from the West and not on threats

---

"Jaruzelski, the Soviet Union, and the Imposition of Martial Law in Poland: New Light on the Mystery of December 1981," *Cold War International History Project Bulletin*, No. 11 (Winter 1998), pp. 5–32; Mark Kramer, "Colonel Kukliński and the Polish Crisis," *Cold War International History Project Bulletin*, No. 11 (Winter 1998), pp. 48–59; Mark Kramer, "'In Case Military Assistance Is Provided to Poland': Soviet Preparations for Military Contingencies, August 1980," *Cold War International History Project Bulletin*, No. 11 (Winter 1998), pp. 102–109; and Mark Kramer, "Poland, 1980–81: Soviet Policy during the Polish Crisis," *Cold War International History Project Bulletin*, No. 5 (Spring 1995), pp. 1, 116–128.

[14] Mark Kramer, "The Soviet Union, the Warsaw Pact, and the Polish Crisis of 1980–1981: Coercion and Delay in Crisis Management," *Journal of Strategic Studies*, forthcoming.

[15] See, for example, "Doświadczenia i wnioski z ćwiczenia 'Mazowsze'," Military Exercise Report (Top Secret – Special Designation), compiled by the Polish General Staff, June 1963, in Archiwum Akt Nowych, Archiwum Komitetu Centralnego PZPR, Sygnatura 5008.

from the East, the Warsaw Pact's strategy prevented those states from developing a defensive capacity against "fraternal" invasions.

Although the intra-bloc policing role of the Warsaw Pact was the alliance's main raison d'être, the Pact also increasingly played a vital role in external defense. From the 1960s through the late 1980s, the Pact served as the primary organ of Soviet and East European war preparations against NATO. The Soviet Union and its allies made elaborate plans and combat preparations for a large-scale "coalition" war against NATO, which would have involved extensive Soviet nuclear strikes as well as joint conventional operations by all Warsaw Pact member-states against NATO forces.

From the early 1970s on, the Warsaw Pact also acquired an important role in political coordination and consultation on a wide range of foreign policy and national security issues. This function proved especially important during the tortuous negotiations in the first half of the 1970s that led to the Final Act of the Conference on Security and Cooperation in Europe (CSCE), signed in Helsinki by thirty-five heads of state in August 1975.[16] During preparations for subsequent CSCE review conferences and for East–West arms control talks in the late 1970s and 1980s, the East European countries exercised considerable influence on political matters within the Warsaw Pact, taking advantage of organizational reforms introduced in 1969 and 1976 that gave them a greater voice.

On military matters, however, the East European members of the Warsaw Pact had much less leeway. Despite a few gestures at reform, the military command structure of the Pact's joint armed forces continued to be dominated by Soviet marshals and generals.[17] Soviet preponderance in the military chain of command was further strengthened in March 1980 by the secret adoption of a "Statute on the Combined Armed Forces of the Warsaw Pact Member-States and Their Command Organs for Wartime," which in the event of war would have placed East European forces under direct Soviet control.[18] Romanian leaders objected to this new statute and declined to go along with it, but all other Pact members

---

[16] See the voluminous declassified Soviet records on CSCE in "Soveshchanie po bezopasnosti i sotrudnichestvu v Evrope: Postanovleniya Politbyuro TsK KPSS s prilozheniyami i materialami, 1969–1975 gg.," in Rossiiskii Gosudarstvennyi Arkhiv Noveishei Istorii (RGANI), Fond (F.) 3, Opis' (Op.) 73; and "Soveshchanie po bezopasnosti i sotrudnichestvu v Evrope: Zapisi besed sotrudnikov sovetskikh posol'stv s gosudarstvennymi i obshchestvennymi deyatelyami i sotrudnikami posol'stv zarubezhnykh stran, 1969–1976 gg.," in RGANI, F. 5, Op. 61, 62, 63, 64, 66, 67, 68, 69.

[17] See, for example, Michael Sadykiewicz, *The Warsaw Pact Command Structure in Peace and War*, RAND Report No. R-3558-RC (Santa Monica, CA: RAND Corporation, September 1988).

[18] U.S. Central Intelligence Agency (CIA), Historical Review Program, *Warsaw Pact Wartime Statutes: Instruments of Control* (Washington, DC: U.S. Government Printing Office, 2011). For the full text of the top-secret wartime statute, adopted on 18 March 1980, see "Grundsätze über die Vereinten Streitkräfte der Teilnehmerstaaten des Warschauer Vertrages und ihr Führungsorgane (für den Krieg)," in BA – Abt. MA, AZN 32854, Ss. 85–120.

signed on, giving Soviet commanders the kind of streamlined control mechanism they deemed necessary for all-out nuclear and conventional war in Europe.

By the time Mikhail Gorbachev became CPSU General Secretary in March 1985, the Warsaw Pact appeared to be a solid organization capable of waging a large-scale war in Europe and conducting operations overseas. The Soviet-led alliance, still under the command of Marshal Kulikov, was a formidable military counterweight to NATO and an effective mechanism of political consensus-building. In late April 1985, Gorbachev and the other Warsaw Pact leaders met in Warsaw to commemorate the thirtieth anniversary of the Pact and agreed to renew it for another thirty years (an initial twenty years plus an automatic ten-year extension). Yet only six years later, on the 1st of July 1991, the Warsaw Pact was formally disbanded, having been rendered obsolete by the political transformation of East-Central Europe over the previous two years – a transformation spurred by a combination of far-reaching change from above (change associated with Gorbachev's "new political thinking"), mass pressure from below, and the sudden loss of will among East European Communist leaders as they increasingly realized that the Soviet Union would no longer strive to maintain orthodox Communist regimes in power throughout the region.

The remarkable events of 1989 in East-Central Europe and the dissolution of the Soviet Union two years later have been analyzed in detail by scholars over the past thirty-five years.[19] The large and burgeoning literature on these topics has focused mainly on political, social, and economic developments, giving scant attention to military issues, including the fate of the Warsaw Pact.[20] Even William

---

[19] A range of perspectives (including my own) on the upheavals of 1989 in the Soviet bloc can be found in Mark Kramer and Vít Smetana, eds., *Imposing, Maintaining, and Tearing Open the Iron Curtain: The Cold War and East-Central Europe, 1945–1990* (Lanham, MD: Rowman & Littlefield, 2013). See also Mark Kramer, "The Demise of the Soviet Bloc," *Journal of Modern History*, Vol. 83, No. 4 (December 2011), pp. 788–854, published in expanded form in Vladimir Tismaneanu and Bogdan C. Iacob, eds., *The End and the Beginning: The Revolutions of 1989 and the Resurgence of History* (Budapest: Central European University Press, 2012), pp. 171–256; Mark Kramer, "The Collapse of East European Communism and the Repercussions within the Soviet Union (Part 3)," *Journal of Cold War Studies*, Vol. 7, No. 1 (Winter 2004–2005), pp. 3–96; Mark Kramer, "The Collapse of East European Communism and the Repercussions within the Soviet Union (Part 2)," *Journal of Cold War Studies*, Vol. 6, No. 4 (Fall 2004), pp. 3–64; and Mark Kramer, "The Collapse of East European Communism and the Repercussions within the Soviet Union (Part 1)," *Journal of Cold War Studies*, Vol. 5, No. 4 (Fall 2003), pp. 178–256.

[20] See, for example, Mark Kramer, "The Dissolution of the Soviet Union: A Case Study in Discontinuous Change," *Journal of Cold War Studies*, Vol. 24, No. 1 (Winter 2021–2022), pp. 188–218; Vladislav M. Zubok, *Collapse: The Fall of the Soviet Union* (New Haven, CT: Yale University Press, 2021); Serhii Plokhy, *The Last Empire: The Final Days of the Soviet Union* (New York: Basic Books, 2014); Archie Brown; *The Human Factor: Gorbachev, Reagan, and Thatcher, and the End of the Cold War* (New York: Oxford University Press, 2020); Stephen Kotkin, *Armageddon Averted: The Soviet Collapse, 1970–2000*, updated ed. (New York: Oxford University Press, 2008); and Mark R. Beissinger, *Nationalist Mobilization and the Collapse of the Soviet State* (New York: Cambridge University Press, 2002).

Odom's book discussing the collapse of the Soviet armed forces devotes very little attention to the Soviet–East European military alliance.[21] Nor has other recent scholarship dealing with the Soviet bloc shed much light on crucial events that precipitated the demise of the Warsaw Pact.

During the Cold War, analysts such as A. Ross Johnson, Thomas Wolfe, Robert W. Dean, Iván Völgyes, James F. Brown, Alexander Alexiev, and David Holloway produced insightful analyses of the Warsaw Pact, focusing especially on the military capabilities and political reliability of the allied armies.[22] Other scholars, such as Andrzej Korbonski, Roger E. Kanet, and Edward Kolodziej, examined the role of the Warsaw Pact in coordinating Soviet and East European policies vis-à-vis the Third World, especially the support that Soviet-bloc countries extended to leftwing guerrilla movements and Marxist-Leninist governments in Africa.[23] Others focused on the political economy of the alliance and the mechanisms of intra-bloc relations.[24] Nearly all of these authors took for granted that the Warsaw Pact would be a permanent fixture in Europe.

---

[21] William E. Odom, *The Collapse of the Soviet Military* (New Haven, CT: Yale University Press, 1998). See also Brian D. Taylor, "The Soviet Military and the Disintegration of the USSR," *Journal of Cold War Studies*, Vol. 5, No. 1 (Winter 2003), pp. 17–66.

[22] A. Ross Johnson, Robert W. Dean, and Alexander Alexiev, *East European Military Establishments: The Warsaw Pact Northern Tier* (New York: Crane, Russak, 1981); Jeffrey Simon, *Warsaw Pact Forces: Problems of Command and Control* (Boulder, CO: Westview Press, 1985); Hugh Faringdon, *Confrontation: The Strategic Geography of NATO and the Warsaw Pact* (London: Routledge, 1986); Arlene Idol Broadhurst, ed., *The Future of European Alliance Systems: NATO and the Warsaw Pact* (Boulder, CO: Westview Press, 1982); Iván Völgyes, *The Political Reliability of the Warsaw Pact Armies: The Southern Tier* (Durham, NC: Duke University Press, 1982); David Holloway and Jane M. O. Sharp, eds., *The Warsaw Pact: Alliance in Transition?* (Ithaca, NY: Cornell University Press, 1984); Daniel N. Nelson, ed., *Soviet Allies: The Warsaw Pact and the Issue of Reliability* (Boulder, CO: Westview Press, 1984); Robert W. Clawson and Lawrence S. Kaplan, eds., *The Warsaw Pact: Political Purpose and Military Means* (Wilmington, DE: Scholarly Resources, 1982); Thomas W. Wolfe, *Soviet Power and Europe, 1945–1970* (Baltimore, MD: Johns Hopkins University Press, 1970); and Mark Kramer, "Civil-Military Relations in the Warsaw Pact: The East European Component," *International Affairs*, Vol. 61, No. 1 (Winter 1985), pp. 45–67.

[23] Roger E. Kanet, ed., *The Soviet Union, Eastern Europe, and the Third World* (New York: Cambridge University Press, 1988); Edward A. Kolodziej and Roger E. Kanet, eds., *The Limits of Soviet Power in the Developing World* (Baltimore, MD: Johns Hopkins University Press, 1989); Roger E. Kanet, "Military Relations between Eastern Europe and Africa," in Bruce E. Arlinghaus, ed., *Arms for Africa: Military Assistance and Foreign Policy in the Developing World* (Lexington, MA: Lexington Books, 1982), pp. 79–99; Andrzej Korbonski and Francis Fukuyama, eds., *The Soviet Union and the Third World: The Last Three Decades* (Ithaca, NY: Cornell University Press, 1987); David Albright and Jiří Valenta, eds., *The Communist States in Africa* (Bloomington, IN: Indiana University Press, 1982); Christopher Coker, *NATO, the Warsaw Pact, and Africa* (Basingstoke: Macmillan, 1985).

[24] Sarah Meiklejohn Terry, ed., *Soviet Policy in Eastern Europe* (New Haven, CT: Yale University Press,1984); Karen Dawisha and Philip Hanson, eds., *Soviet-East European Dilemmas: Coercion, Competition, and Consent* (London: Holmes & Meier, 1981); Gerald Holden, *The Warsaw Pact: Soviet Security and Bloc Politics* (Oxford: Blackwell Books, 1989); Charles Gati, *Hungary and the Soviet Bloc* (Durham, NC: Duke University Press, 1986); Jonathan Eyal, ed.,

After the Cold War ended, the declassification of archival materials in former East-bloc countries and the publication of memoirs and interviews with former officials enabled scholars to produce much richer and more detailed studies of the Warsaw Pact, including the changes in the late 1980s that undermined the raison d'être and political underpinnings of the alliance. Although relatively little new scholarship on the matter appeared in the 1990s, this was mainly because researchers were just starting to delve into the vast body of evidence that had suddenly become available. The initial post-1989 literature on the Warsaw Pact consisted mainly of items drawing on materials stored in the former East German military archives and Communist party archives, which revealed a great deal about Warsaw Pact military planning and exercises, including the heavy emphasis placed by Soviet military commanders on the early wartime use of nuclear missile strikes.[25]

In the 2000s, pathbreaking work began appearing after the start of a multi-country effort known as the Parallel History Project on NATO and the Warsaw Pact (PHP), launched in 1999 by Vojtech Mastny.[26] For roughly a decade starting in 2000, the PHP collected copies of large quantities of declassified documents from former Warsaw Pact countries (and from some NATO countries) and made them available online. These collections complemented, and went well beyond, the voluminous declassified Soviet-bloc records obtained since the early 1990s by the DC-based Cold War International History Project of the Woodrow Wilson International Center for Scholars.

The PHP not only gathered declassified materials but also sponsored the publication of anthologies of translated documents and analytical essays as well as oral history transcripts.[27] Especially noteworthy was a lengthy volume

---

The Warsaw Pact and the Balkans: Moscow's Southern Flank (Basingstoke: Macmillan, 1989); and Christopher D. Jones, *Soviet Influence in Eastern Europe: Political Autonomy and the Warsaw Pact* (New York: Pergamon, 1981).

[25] Among early items based on declassified East German military and party archival documents, see Mark Kramer, "Warsaw Pact Military Planning in Central Europe: Revelations from the East German Archives," *Cold War International History Project Bulletin*, No. 2 (Fall 1992), pp. 1, 13–19; Beatrice Heuser, "Warsaw Pact Military Doctrines in the 1970s and 1980s: Findings in the East German Archives," *Comparative Strategy*, Vol. 12, No. 4 (October–December 1993), pp. 437–457; and Christoph Bluth, "The Warsaw Pact and Military Security in Central Europe during the Cold War," *Journal of Slavic Military Studies*, Vol. 17, No. 2 (April 2004), pp. 299–331.

[26] The PHP was renamed the Parallel History Project on Collective Security after the Swiss Federal Institute of Technology in Zurich (ETH-Zurich) took it over in 2007. The PHP ceased to function in 2011, but ETH-Zurich has maintained the online collections on its website (www.isn.eth.ch/php).

[27] Vojtech Mastny, Sven Holtsmark, and Andreas Wenger, eds., *War Plans and Alliances in the Cold War: Threat Perceptions in the East and West* (New York: Routledge, 2006); Andreas Wenger, Vojtech Mastny, and Christian Nuenlist, eds., *Origins of the European Security System: The Helsinki Process Revisited 1965–75* (New York: Routledge, 2008); and

offering a document-based history of the Warsaw Pact from 1955 to 1991 compiled by Mastny and Malcolm Byrne of the National Security Archive. The volume, published in 2005, included translations of documents collected from all the former Warsaw Pact countries along with a lucid introduction and valuable headnotes by the editors.[28]

More recently, several books published in Germany (mostly edited collections) have drawn on declassified archival records to offer cogent insights into the military and political dimensions of the Warsaw Pact, including the alliance's final years.[29] Especially valuable in this regard is a brief monograph by Gerhard Wettig, *Gorbatschow: Reformpolitik und Warschauer Pakt, 1985–1991*, published in Austria in 2021 with support from the Ludwig Boltzmann Institute for the Study of War's Consequences.[30] Wettig, a prominent German researcher who retired two decades ago but has continued to produce illuminating work, draws very well on scholarship of mine and on declassified documents from the German and former Soviet archives that I co-edited in two large volumes with three researchers from the Boltzmann Institute and from Germany in 2014 and 2015.[31]

A book published by Laurien Crump of Utrecht University in 2016 examines the first fifteen years of the Warsaw Pact based in part on recently declassified East-bloc materials. Crump's book covers this early period well, but she mostly corroborates and reinforces what earlier analyses had shown. The corroboration the book provides is very important, but overall it breaks relatively little new ground and ends long before the period covered here.[32] Of greater relevance to

---

Jan Hoffenaar and Christopher Findlay, eds., *Military Planning for European Theatre Conflict in the Cold War: An Oral History Roundtable* (Zurich: Center for Security Studies, ETH-Zurich, 2007).

[28] Vojtech Mastny and Malcolm Byrne, eds., *A Cardboard Castle? An Inside History of the Warsaw Pact, 1955–1991* (Budapest: Central European University Press, 2005).

[29] Hans-Hubertus Mack, László Veszprémy, and Rüdiger Wenzke, *Die NVA und die Ungarische Volksarmee im Warschauer Pakt* (Potsdam: Militärgeschichtliches Forschungsamt, 2019); Rüdiger Wenzke, ed., *Die Streitkräfte der DDR und Polens in der Operationsplanung des Warschauer Paktes* (Potsdam: Militärgeschichtliches Forschungsamt, 2010); Torsten Diedrich, Winfried Heinemann, and Christian F. Ostermann, eds., *Der Warschauer Pakt: Von der Gründung bis zum Zusammenbruch 1955 bis 1991* (Berlin: Ch. Links Verlag, 2009); and Frank Umbach, *Das rote Bündnis: Entwicklung und Zerfall des Warschauer Pakts 1955–1991* (Berlin: Ch. Links Verlag, 2005).

[30] Gerhard Wettig, *Gorbatschow: Reformpolitik und Warschauer Pakt, 1985–1991* (Innsbruck: Studien Verlag, 2021).

[31] Stefan Karner, Mark Kramer, Peter Ruggenthaler, and Manfred Wilke, eds., *Der Kreml und die Wende 1989: Interne Analysen der sowjetischen Führung zum Fall der kommunistischen Regime – Dokumente* (Innsbruck: Studien Verlag, 2014); and Stefan Karner, Mark Kramer, Peter Ruggenthaler, and Manfred Wilke, eds., *Der Kreml und die deutsche Wiedervereinigung 1990: Interne sowjetische Analysen* (Berlin: Metropol, 2015).

[32] Laurien Crump, *The Warsaw Pact Reconsidered: International Relations in Eastern Europe, 1955–69* (New York: Routledge, 2015).

my discussion in this Element is a two-volume history of the Warsaw Pact published by the Czech scholar Matěj Bílý in 2016 and 2021, based primarily on materials from the former Czechoslovak archives.[33] Bílý's first volume picks up where Crump's book leaves off, looking at the 1970s and the first half of the 1980s. Bílý's second volume, which is especially relevant to the discussion here, recounts the final six years of the Warsaw Pact, showing how the alliance initially seemed to be functioning normally but then came unraveled much faster and more decisively than almost anyone had anticipated. Insightful though Bílý's book is, it does not adequately discuss certain key actions in both the USSR and several East-Central European countries that helped to precipitate social and political upheavals in the region and the subsequent demise of the Warsaw Pact.

An analysis that takes fuller account of important policy changes, as well as the role of contingency and chance, was published by the Hungarian scholar Csaba Békés in 2023 that traces how Hungary and other East European members of the Warsaw Pact acted individually and in concert in 1990–1991 to ensure that the Warsaw Pact would come to an end.[34] The East European governments, as Békés recounts, had to act firmly to circumvent the efforts of Soviet leaders to preserve the organization. Another aspect of the story – the impact on the Warsaw Pact of East Germany's departure from the alliance in September 1990, shortly before Germany was formally reunified – has been discussed very well by Susanne Maslanka in an article published in 2022 that draws extensively on declassified West German records, memoirs, and some translated Soviet materials.[35]

Newly released Soviet-bloc documents have also enabled scholars to expand on earlier work about the role of the Warsaw Pact in facilitating Soviet and East European activities in Third World countries, including weapons transfers, internal security training, and military support. Numerous edited collections, monographs, and articles on the topic have highlighted the important ways that

---

[33] Matěj Bílý, *Varšavská smlouva 1969–1985: Vrchol a cesta k zániku* (Prague: Ústav pro studium totalitních režimů, 2016); and Matěj Bílý, *Varšavská smlouva 1985–1991: Dezintegrace a rozpad* (Prague: Ústav pro studium totalitních režimů, 2021). The two volumes have recently appeared in English translation: *The Warsaw Pact 1969–1985: The Pinnacle and Path to Dissolution* (London: Academica Press, 2020); and *The Warsaw Pact, 1985–1991: Disintegration and Dissolution* (New York: Routledge, 2023).

[34] Csaba Békés, "Hungary and the Dissolution of the Warsaw Pact (1988–1991)," *Journal of Cold War Studies*, Vol. 25, No. 4 (Fall 2023), pp. 4–23. Another article covering some of the same ground is Simon Miles, "We All Fall Down: The Dismantling of the Warsaw Pact and the End of the Cold War in Eastern Europe," *International Security*, Vol. 48, No. 3 (Winter 2023/24), pp. 51–85.

[35] Susanne Maslanka, "The Withdrawal of the GDR from the Warsaw Pact: Expectations, Hopes, and Disappointments in German-Soviet Relations during the Dissociation Process," *Historical Social Research*, Vol. 47, No. 2 (2022), pp. 53–76.

East European governments used the Pact as a foreign policy mechanism, working in conjunction with the Soviet Union.[36] These recent publications, which have also underscored the role of Cuba in its dealings with Warsaw Pact countries in the Third World, have enriched and corroborated the findings of scholarship produced in the 1970s and 1980s, before the Cold War ended.

Although the latest scholarship has filled important gaps, an integrated account of the political and military changes that culminated in the dissolution of the Warsaw Pact is still needed, particularly in tracing the key decisions in Moscow that ultimately determined the fate of the alliance. Drawing on declassified archival documents and publications from the countries of the former Soviet bloc, this Cambridge Element highlights the various attempts from 1985 to mid-1989 to carry out reforms in the Warsaw Pact and to adapt the alliance to Gorbachev's "new thinking" in Soviet foreign policy, especially to the goals of "reasonable defense sufficiency" and "non-offensive defense." The analysis here sets this process in the broader context of the reorientation of Soviet policy toward Eastern Europe under Gorbachev, whose role in adopting new policies was so crucial and had such profound consequences that it is emphasized throughout the text. Because major changes in military structures and deployments can often take years to carry out, the Warsaw Pact as an organization was still largely intact by the time the upheavals of 1989 altered the entire political complexion of Eastern Europe and undermined the raison d'être of the alliance. Despite a flurry of efforts by Soviet officials in 1990 to preserve the Warsaw Pact and convert it into a mainly political entity, the fate of the organization was sealed by the events of 1989.

Early Signs of Continuity and Change

For more than a year after Gorbachev came to power, Soviet policy vis-à-vis the Warsaw Pact seemed to be largely a continuation of the past. On March 6, 1985, a few days before Gorbachev was elevated to the post of CPSU General Secretary, he delivered the keynote speech to a closed gathering of high-level Communist party officials from the Warsaw Pact countries. Echoing previous

---

[36] Philip E. Muehlenbeck and Natalia Telepneva, eds., *Warsaw Pact Intervention in the Third World: Aid and Influence in the Cold War* (London: I.B. Tauris, 2018); Chris Saunders, Helder Adegar Fonseca, and Lena Dallywater, eds., *Eastern Europe, the Soviet Union, and Africa: New Perspectives on the Era of Decolonization, 1950s to 1990s* (Oldenbourg: De Gruyter, 2023); Klaus Storkmann, *Geheime Solidarität: Militärbeziehungen und Militärhilfen der DDR in die Dritte Welt* (Berlin: Christoph Links Verlag, 2012); Klaus Storkmann, "East German Military Aid to the Sandinista Government of Nicaragua, 1979–1990," *Journal of Cold War Studies*, Vol. 16, No. 2 (Spring 2014), pp. 56–76; and Klaus Storkmann, "East Germany as Player in the 'Global Cold War'? East Germany's Military Commitment to Africa and the Middle East, and Its Coordination with the Soviet Leadership," *Revista de istorie militară* (Bucharest), No. 3 (2019), pp. 111–125.

Soviet leaders' orthodox views about the Warsaw Pact, he told the assembled officials that "in relations between our fraternal parties we have been consistently and unwaveringly implementing the principles of socialist internationalism. This is a great accomplishment of the fraternal parties, who are united by a commonality of ideals and means of struggle."[37] Gorbachev warned that the Soviet bloc was confronted by the "insidious designs" of NATO:

> Imperialism in recent years has coordinated its actions against the socialist states. This coordination has spread to all spheres – political, military, economic, and ideological.... Imperialism is trying to dissipate our unity and impose alien views, morals, economic and political standards, and models of development. Their apologists prattle on about "bridge-building" and about freedom and human rights. They spread false ideas and tell lies for one purpose only: to shake our unity, weaken us, and remove the main barrier to the fulfillment of imperialist intrigues.

He emphasized that the Warsaw Pact member-states would "have to achieve ever greater coordination of our work" and "deal a decisive rebuff to ... the real danger of imperialism's militaristic course" and the "stepped-up efforts by our enemies" to "sow divisions within our ranks."[38]

On March 11, 1985, right after Gorbachev was appointed CPSU General Secretary, he continued to stress the need for tighter unity in the Warsaw Pact, pledging that his "first priority" in foreign policy would be "to protect and strengthen as much as possible the fraternal friendship with our closest comrades-in-arms and allies, the countries of the great socialist commonwealth."[39] Elaborating on this theme at an important plenum of the CPSU Central Committee the following month, Gorbachev called for "the improvement and enrichment of cooperation among the fraternal socialist countries in every possible way, the development of comprehensive ties, the assurance of close collaboration in the political, economic, ideological, military, and other spheres, and the organic merger of the national and international interests of all members of the great [socialist] commonwealth."[40] The official Soviet TASS

---

[37] "Vstrecha sekretarei Tsentral'nykh Komitetov bratskikh partii sotsialisticheskikh stran po ideologii i propaganda, Moskva, 6 marta 1985 goda: Stenogramma pervogo (utrennego) zasedaniya," Marked-up Verbatim Proceedings (Top Secret), March 6, 1985, in RGANI, F. 10, Op. 1, D. 548, L. 1.

[38] Ibid., Ll. 10–11.

[39] "Rech' General'nogo sekretarya TsK KPSS tovarishcha M.S. Gorbacheva na Plenume TsK KPSS 11 marta 1985 goda," *Pravda* (Moscow), March 12, 1985, p. 3.

[40] "Plenum Tsentral'nogo Komiteta TsK KPSS, 22–23 aprelya 1985 goda," April 22–23, 1985 (Top Secret), in RGANI, F. 2, Op. 3, Delo (D.) 347, List (L.) 12. Gorbachev's speech was published the next day as "O sozyve ocherednogo XXVII S"ezda KPSS i zadachakh svyazannykh s ego podgotovkoi i provedeniem: Doklad General'nogo sekretarya TsK KPSS M. S. Gorbacheva," *Pravda* (Moscow), 23 1985, p. 2.

press agency prominently highlighted these comments in dispatches it provided to the domestic Soviet press and for wire-service distribution abroad.

A few days later, on April 26, when Gorbachev and the other East-bloc leaders gathered in Poland to extend the Warsaw Pact for an additional thirty years, the participants issued a joint communiqué vowing to "increase their close cooperation in international affairs" and "reinforce their efforts to strengthen the combat cohesion of the alliance."[41] Nothing more about the proceedings was released at the time, but the declassified records show that Gorbachev, in his keynote speech at the meeting, praised the "unity of action" that had "thwarted the attempts by imperialism to subvert or 'destroy' the socialist order in any of the fraternal countries," a clear reference to the events of 1968 and 1980–1981 when challenges to Communist regimes in Eastern Europe were forcibly suppressed.[42] Gorbachev also lauded "our joint efforts in accomplishing a task of historic importance – we have reached military-strategic parity with NATO. This was not at all easy to do." He made clear that the Warsaw Pact must never fall behind in its ability to "wage an active fight against the military threat" from NATO:

> Military-strategic parity is a vital prerequisite for the security of the socialist states. Understandably, safeguarding the military balance has required – and, if the situation does not improve, will continue to require – a great deal of resources and effort. But without this it will be impossible to defend socialist gains. This is our common affair, the success of which will depend on contributions from every socialist state.[43]

Far from displaying any inclination to relax Soviet military–political ties with the East European countries, Gorbachev strongly emphasized the need for "a unified line" and "stricter coordination of efforts" to "consolidate the position of socialism."[44] His insistence that the treaty be extended by thirty years rather than a much shorter period (of perhaps five to ten years) as some East European

---

[41] "Kommyunike o vstreche vysshikh partiinykh i gosudarstvennykh deyatelei stran-uchastnits Varshavskogo Dogovora," *Krasnaya zvezda* (Moscow), April 27, 1985, pp. 1–2.

[42] The passages quoted here are from the verbatim text of Gorbachev's speech, with corrections marked in by hand, "Vystuplenie General'nogo sekretarya TsK KPSS M. S. Gorbacheva na vstreche 26 aprelya 1985 goda: Teksty okonchatel'nyi s redaktsionnymi pravkami," Stenogram (Top Secret), in RGANI, F. 10, Op. 3, D. 149, Ll. 1–44 (the final text is on Ll. 1–14, and the mark-ups are on Ll. 15–44). For a Czech version of Gorbachev's speech, translated from the original Russian, see "Vystoupení generálního tajemníka ÚV Komunistické strany Sovětského svazu soudruha M. S. Gorbačova: Příloha IV/d," April 26, 1985, 8696/24, in Národní archiv České republiky (NA ČR), Archiv Ústředního výboru Komunistické strany Československa (Arch. ÚV KSČ), PÚV 47/85, Listí (Ll.) 1–11.

[43] "Vystuplenie General'nogo sekretarya TsK KPSS M. S. Gorbacheva na vstreche 26 aprelya 1985 goda," L. 2.

[44] Ibid., L. 8.

officials had wanted, and his determination to prevent any changes in the basic text of the treaty (or in the top-secret supplementary Provisions on the Unified Command of the Armed Forces of the Member-States of the Warsaw Pact, which were to be implemented during a crisis or war), underscored his desire to push for greater cohesion and integration between the USSR and its allies.

This same approach, with its echoes of the policies adopted by previous Soviet leaders toward Eastern Europe, was evident during other high-level deliberations in Moscow in 1985 and 1986. At CPSU Politburo meetings, Gorbachev called for an expansion of political and military ties within the Warsaw Pact and promised to safeguard the "underlying path of development of our cooperation with the other socialist countries."[45] Newly available archival evidence contravenes the speculation by a few Western analysts that Gorbachev decided at an early stage to leave the East European states to their own devices. The transcripts of Soviet Politburo meetings and other secret discussions from 1985 and 1986 show nothing of the sort.[46] Rather than proposing to loosen Moscow's relations with the East European states, Gorbachev during this period not only wanted to establish "greater [Communist] party control" over Soviet–East European relations but also sought to "strengthen the unity of the socialist countries and to counter any centrifugal tendencies" within the Warsaw Pact.[47] Although he said it would be pointless to

---

[45] "Zasedanie Politbyuro TsK KPSS 26 iyunya 1986 goda: Zapiska tov. Gorbacheva M. S. o nekotorykh aktual'nykh voprosakh sotrudnichestva s sotsialisticheskimi stranami," Politburo Protocol No. 18 (Top Secret), June 26, 1986, in RGANI, F. 89, Op. 36, D. 19, L. 1.

[46] Notes from CPSU Politburo meetings and many other high-level discussions from 1985 to 1991 were gathered in 2003–2004 by the Gorbachev Foundation for a planned five-volume documentary collection titled *Kak "delalas'" politika perestroiki* (KDPP) that originally was slated to appear in 2004. Unfortunately, Gorbachev decided not to publish the volumes, which would have come to more than 3,500 pages in total. Later on he did permit a much abridged single volume to appear – A. Chernyaev, ed., *V Politbyuro TsK KPSS: Po zapisyam Anatoliya Chernyaeva, Vadima Medvedeva, Georgiya Shakhnazarova* (Moscow: Al'pina Biznes-Buks, 2006) – as well as a collection of documents pertaining to Soviet policy in Germany: Aleksandr Galkin and Anatolii Chernyaev, eds., *Mikhail Gorbachev i germanskii vopros: Sbornik dokumentov, 1986–1991* (Moscow: Ves' mir, 2006). In 2010, another thick volume was published with transcripts and materials from Gorbachev's conversations with foreign leaders – A. S. Chernyaev and A. B. Veber, eds., *Otvechaya na vyzov vremeni: Vneshnya politika perestroiki – Dokumental'nye svidetel'stva* (Moscow: Ves' mir, 2010) – but the other documents planned for KDPP have not yet been made generally available. Fortunately, the late Anatolii Chernyaev, who oversaw the project and would have preferred to release all of the materials, agreed to give me (as well as other researchers) access to the unpublished volumes when I was in Moscow numerous times from 2005 to 2009. I am grateful to Chernyaev for the opportunity to go through all the documents. Copies of the documents are available in the Cold War Studies archival collection at Harvard University For my analysis here, I have supplemented the Gorbachev Foundation documents with other Politburo transcripts that are available at RGANI in Moscow (in Fond 89) or that were given to me by the late General Dmitrii Volkogonov.

[47] "V Politbyuro TsK KPSS: O nekotorykh aktual'nykh voprosakh sotrudnichestva s sotsstranami," Memorandum from M. S. Gorbachev to the CPSU Politburo, June 25, 1986 (Secret), supplement

treat the East European states like "little children who need to be brought to kindergarten," he was convinced that the Soviet Union's "objective interests demand unity and cohesion among the countries of socialism" as well as "comprehensive coordination of all foreign policy actions." The East European governments, he argued, "know that any initiative they put forth must enjoy our [Soviet] support and must be coordinated with us, or else it will never get anywhere and will be doomed from the start."[48] Gorbachev assured his colleagues on the CPSU Politburo that the Soviet Union would continue to be, as it had been under his predecessors, "the leader of the socialist world and the [military] guarantor of the security and socialist gains of all the fraternal countries."[49]

Gorbachev expressed similar views when he spoke with East European leaders. In a series of bilateral and multilateral meetings with high-ranking East European officials in 1985 and early 1986, Gorbachev urged them to pursue closer military, political, and economic integration with the Soviet Union. In 1985 alone, five separate gatherings of Warsaw Pact leaders were convened, including two in March, one in late April, one in early October, and one in November shortly after Gorbachev returned from his first summit meeting with Ronald Reagan in Geneva. Gorbachev assured the East European leaders that the Soviet Union would show "respect for [their countries'] experience and understanding of [their] national specifics" and would support their "quest to follow national paths" to socialism. But in making these pledges, he hoped to facilitate, rather than impede, the "strengthening of our cooperation, cohesion, and unity." Gorbachev left no doubt that his primary aim was to "develop comprehensive cooperation on all matters with the countries of the socialist commonwealth" – a goal that was fully consistent with earlier Soviet policies.[50]

In public as well, Gorbachev's initial statements about Eastern Europe seemed to be in full accord with the basic policies devised under his predecessors. The new Soviet leader's manner of presentation was more dynamic and innovative, but at no time during his first years in office did he disavow the Brezhnev Doctrine or express any negative comments about Soviet policy during the crises of 1956, 1968, and 1980–1981. In retrospect, what Gorbachev said at the 27th Soviet Party

---

to Point 1 of Politburo Protocol No. 18, in Arkhiv Prezidenta Rossiiskoi Federatsii (APRF), F. 3, Op. 102, D. 218, Ll. 4, 5.

[48] The quoted passages here and in the previous sentence are from Gorbachev's keynote speech to a closed meeting of the Soviet Foreign Ministry Collegium, May 28, 1986, declassified and published in M. S. Gorbachev, *Gody trudnykh reshenii* (Moscow: Al'fa-print, 1993), pp. 46–55.

[49] "V Politbyuro TsK KPSS: O nekotorykh aktual'nykh voprosakh sotrudnichestva s sotsstranami," L. 5.

[50] "Niederschrift über das Treffen der Generalsekretäre und Ersten Sekretäre der Zentralkomitees der Bruderparteien der Teilnehmerstaaten des Warschauer Vertrages am 23. Oktober 1985 in Sofia," Stenographic Transcript, October 23, 1985 (Top Secret), in Stiftung Archiv der Parteien und Massenorganisationen der DDR im Bundesarchiv (SAPMO-BA), Zentrales Parteiarchiv (ZPA), IV 2/1/638.

Congress in February 1986, in a report devoted mainly to economic reform and other domestic matters, appears more significant than it did at the time. He advocated "unconditional respect in international practice for the right of every people to choose the paths and forms of its development," and he refrained from mentioning the concept of "socialist internationalism."[51] In addition, he declared that "the unity [of the Warsaw Pact countries] has nothing in common with uniformity, hierarchy, interference by some parties in the affairs of others, or the striving of any party to have a monopoly on what is right," adding that all Soviet-bloc countries should display a "considerate and respectful attitude to each other's experience and put such experience to practical use."[52] Significant though these statements may appear in retrospect, they did not actually go beyond what Nikita Khrushchev had said thirty years earlier, shortly before he approved the invasion of Hungary. Moreover, the new CPSU Program that was adopted at the 27th Soviet Party Congress, unlike Gorbachev's speech, spoke explicitly about the need for "mutual assistance" and "constant vigilance" in "defending socialist gains" and about the paramount importance of "socialist internationalism" for the Soviet bloc – the essence of the Brezhnev Doctrine.[53]

The mixed signals coming from the 27th Party Congress reflected Gorbachev's own cautious sentiments at the time, particularly his desire to proceed gradually and avoid letting events get out of hand in Eastern Europe while he was trying to deal with many other matters both at home and abroad. By all accounts, the lessons of the mid-1950s played a role here. In February 1956, Khrushchev launched his de-Stalinization campaign at the 20th Soviet Party Congress, which effectively undercut the position of many East European leaders and sparked a surge of popular unrest and turmoil throughout the region. Political opposition in Eastern Europe became intertwined with the economic grievances that had accumulated both during the Stalin era and after.

In the meantime, Soviet leaders, being preoccupied with domestic affairs and political maneuvering in the Kremlin, were largely oblivious to the explosive situation that was developing. In June 1956 a violent rebellion erupted in Poland, and this was followed four months later by a violent revolution in Hungary, which Soviet troops eventually crushed via a large-scale invasion. To

---

[51] "Politicheskii doklad Tsentral'nogo Komiteta KPSS XXVII S"ezdu Kommunisticheskoi partii Sovetskogo Soyuza: Doklad General'nogo sekretarya TsK KPSS tovarishcha Gorbacheva M. S.," *Pravda* (Moscow), February 26, 1986, pp. 2–10. Indeed, the speech limited the Soviet Union's "internationalist duty" to that of setting a positive example for other countries by achieving "advances in the development of socialism" at home.

[52] Ibid., Ll. 7, 9. The earlier drafts of Gorbachev's speech, stored in RGANI, F. 1, Op. 3, Dd. 348 –350, show only very minor changes in the wording of these passages – changes of no substantive import.

[53] "Programma Kommunisticheskoi partii Sovetskogo Soyuza," *Pravda* (Moscow), March 7, 1986, p. 7.

avoid a repetition of this earlier pattern, Gorbachev was careful when he offered support for political reform in Eastern Europe during his initial years in office. Unlike Khrushchev, he avoided making statements or taking rash actions that would create a temptation for people in the East European countries to challenge Communist rule or to seek an end to Soviet hegemony in the region.

In the months following the 27th Soviet Party Congress, Soviet policy vis-à-vis the Warsaw Pact continued to reflect these diverging sentiments of caution and reform. On the one hand, Gorbachev repeatedly stressed the need for increased discipline and cohesion in the Soviet bloc, a theme he voiced both at a meeting of the Warsaw Pact's Political Consultative Committee (PCC) in June 1986 and at the 10th Congress of the Polish United Workers' Party (PZPR) a few weeks later. At the PCC meeting, he called for "increasingly close cooperation among the socialist countries" and highlighted the "great need for an increase in common action."[54] At the PZPR congress, Gorbachev argued that the development of "cooperative links among the socialist countries" should be given "absolute priority" and that those links should extend to all areas – "political, economic, cultural, and military."[55] He also seemed to provide a thinly veiled reaffirmation of the Brezhnev Doctrine when he warned that "socialist gains are irreversible" and that any attempt by internal or external forces to "wrench a country away from the socialist commonwealth would mean encroaching not only on the will of the people [in that country], but also on the entire postwar order and, in the final analysis, on peace." His lengthy comments supporting the Polish Communist regime's sweeping crackdown on Solidarity (the "internal enemies of socialist Poland") and imposition of martial law in December 1981 reinforced the point.

On the other hand, some seemingly modest steps that went largely unnoticed laid the groundwork for more sweeping changes in the years ahead. The appointment in March 1986 of Vadim Medvedev as the CPSU Secretary responsible for intra-bloc affairs, replacing Konstantin Rusakov (who had held the post since 1977), brought in an official on whom Gorbachev could rely to instill greater flexibility into the CPSU Department for Ties with Communist and Workers' Parties of Socialist Countries, the body most directly responsible for policy toward East-Central Europe.[56] In September 1986, Medvedev designated Georgii Shakhnazarov, the long-time deputy head of the CPSU Department for Ties with Communist and Workers' Parties, to

---

[54] "Niederschrift über die interne Beratung der Generalsekretäre und Ersten Sekretäre der Bruderparteien der Mitgliedsstaaten des Warschauer Vertrages am 11. 6. 1986 in Budapest," Stenographic Transcript (Top Secret), June 11, 1986, in SAPMO, DY/30/2353, Blatt (Bl.) 11.

[55] "X Zjazd Polskiej Zjednoczonej Partii Robotniczej – wystąpienie tow. Gorbaczowa M. S.," *Trybuna Ludu* (Warsaw), July 1, 1986, p. 1.

[56] See Medvedev's first-hand account, *Raspad: Kak on nazreval v "mirovoi sisteme sotsializma"* (Moscow: Mezhdunarodnye otnosheniya, 1994).

become the first deputy head in place of Oleg Rakhmanin. Shakhnazarov at the time was already known as a reform-minded official, and he subsequently (from 1988) proved to be one of the chief advisers to Gorbachev on Soviet policy toward Eastern Europe and a key figure in restructuring the Warsaw Pact.

More important, the official whom Shakhnazarov replaced, Rakhmanin, was a notorious hardliner who had published an article in *Pravda* in June 1985 that cast a pall on Soviet–East European relations.[57] The article warned the East European governments not to adopt any market-oriented economic reforms or political measures that would "compromise Marxism-Leninism as the basis of the fraternal states' unity" and "distort the general laws of socialist construction." The article also repeatedly stressed the "common responsibility of all the socialist countries for the fate of world socialism" and declared that "on all major international issues the foreign policy of the USSR and of the Marxist-Leninist core of world socialism is identical." One of Gorbachev's closest aides, Anatolii Chernyaev, later wrote that the Soviet leader was deeply irritated by the unexpected appearance of Rakhmanin's article, which apparently was published without authorization from high levels.[58] At a CPSU Politburo meeting a week after the article appeared, Gorbachev voiced his displeasure and rebuked Rakhmanin's superiors. Although Gorbachev decided not to remove Rakhmanin immediately, the eventual appointment of Shakhnazarov as the new first deputy chief of the intra-bloc department was a clear signal that Soviet policy would be changing.

Shakhnazarov's promotion was accompanied by a notable if small change in the Warsaw Pact, namely, the leeway given to East European governments to permit the mass media to cover problems that arose with Soviet military forces stationed on East European soil, a shift in line with Gorbachev's newly proclaimed policy of *glasnost* (greater official openness, especially in the press) in the USSR. In the pre-Gorbachev era, negative aspects of the Soviet Union's military presence in Eastern Europe were a taboo subject, but starting in August 1986, when the Hungarian authorities allowed a report to be published about an accident involving Soviet troops, coverage of such incidents became increasingly common in the East European mass media.[59] Although East European news outlets also took pains to highlight the "positive

---

[57] The article was published pseudonymously as O. Vladimirov, "Vedushchii faktor mirovogo revolyutsionnogo protsessa," *Pravda* (Moscow), June 21, 1985, pp. 3–4.

[58] A. S. Chernyaev, *Shest' let s Gorbachevym: Po dnevnikovym zapisyam* (Moscow: Progress-Kul'tura, 1993), pp. 49–51. Chernyaev's account contains two minor mistakes, giving Rakhmanin's surname as Rakhmaninov and referring to July instead of June.

[59] "Ahonnan nem lehet elmenekülni, az ország peremén," *Heti Világgazdaság* (Budapest), No. 36 (August 16, 1986), pp. 7–8. See also Jeremy King, "The Partial Soviet Troop Withdrawal from Hungary," *RAD Background Report* 166 (Munich: Radio Free Europe Research, September 11, 1989), p. 4.

work" of Soviet forces and the "fraternal aid" they provided (e.g., helping out with snow removal or with gathering the harvest), and although some aspects of the Soviet military presence in Eastern Europe (e.g., financial costs, environmental damage, deployments of nuclear weapons, chains of command) were still off-limits, the appearance of news reports about long-standing problems with Soviet troops, including crimes committed by Soviet personnel, marked a striking departure. Complaints in Hungary about excessive noise caused by low-flying Soviet military aircraft even spurred Soviet commanders to set stricter limits on the hours of flight, and similar complaints in Czechoslovakia induced a Soviet aviation unit to relocate to a site further away from inhabited areas. Before long, the USSR's own press also began covering problems with Soviet air and ground forces stationed in East European countries.[60]

Nevertheless, this trend toward somewhat greater openness, which led eventually (in March 1988) to the creation of a Warsaw Pact press and information office akin to the public affairs office operated by NATO since the time it was founded, did not dispel the uncertainty associated with the conflicting strands of Soviet policy vis-à-vis Eastern Europe. Much of the residue of the past remained. When the Warsaw Pact's Military Council met in November 1986, Marshal Kulikov told the East European participants that the "growing danger of war" with NATO "compels us to adopt measures that will bolster the security of our countries and our peoples and to increase the combat readiness of the armed forces of the Warsaw Pact member-states."[61]

The following month, at a meeting of the Pact's Council of Defense Ministers, a Soviet deputy defense minister, Army-General Evgenii Ivanovskii, reported that the Soviet Union planned to "deploy airborne assault forces on a wide scale [in allied countries] in order to give a more dynamic character to [the Warsaw Pact's joint] offensive operations."[62] In subsequent months, the Soviet defense minister, Marshal Sergei Sokolov, repeatedly vowed both publicly and privately that the Warsaw Pact countries would "never under any circumstances permit [NATO] to gain military superiority" over them. Sokolov emphasized that the USSR and its

---

[60] See, for example, "Strakh pered morozom,"*Izvestiya* (Moscow), March 17, 1987, p. 3.
[61] "Wesentlicher Inhalt der Ausführungen des Oberkommandierenden der Vereinten Streitkräfte zu den Ergebnissen und Schlußfolgerungen, die sich aus dem Treffen in Reykjavik ergeben," GVS No. A-470 410 (Top Secret), November 10, 1986, in Bundesarchiv – Abteilung Militärarchiv (BA – Abt. MA), VA-01/32647, Bl. 2.
[62] Thesen zum Vortrag des Oberbefehlshabers der Landstreitkräfte und Stellvertreters des Ministers für Verteidigung der UdSSR, Armeegeneral J. F. Iwanowski, auf der 19. Sitzung des Komitees der Verteidigungsminister der Teilnehmerstaaten des Warschauer Vertrages zum dritten Tagesordnungspunkt 'Schaffung und Gefechtseinsatz der Luftsturmtruppen under der Marineinfanterie in den verbündeten Armeen und Flotten'," VVS-No. A 470 389 (Top Secret), December 1–3, 1986, in BA – Abt. MA, DVW 1/7 1046, Bl. 2.

allies would have to maintain a permanent "high level of combat readiness," and he urged the East European states to contribute more to joint defense efforts – a demand that caused dismay in Warsaw Pact capitals.[63]

Gorbachev himself remained cautious in his statements and actions vis-à-vis the Warsaw Pact during the first part of 1987, both publicly and privately. When he met with senior East European officials in a closed session in mid-February 1987, he assured them that the Soviet Union "will not impose its own policies on anyone and will not call on you to act like us. We will, however, hope for solidarity and for understanding."[64] He echoed these sentiments two months later during a long-awaited visit to Czechoslovakia, his first trip there since becoming General Secretary of the CPSU. In his main public speech in Prague, Gorbachev declared that the Soviet Union was not "calling on anyone to imitate us. Every socialist country has its own specific features, and the fraternal [Communist] parties determine their political line with an eye to their own national conditions." He insisted that "the entire system of political relations between the socialist countries can and must be based unswervingly on a foundation of equality and mutual responsibility," and he pledged that the Soviet Union would not "claim a special status in the socialist world" or encroach on the "independence of every [Communist] party, its responsibility to its people, and its right to resolve its own country's problems of development in a sovereign way."[65]

In each case, however, Gorbachev qualified these assertions with language reminiscent of the Brezhnev Doctrine. After stating that the Soviet Union would not seek to impose its ideas of reform on other countries, he added: "At the same time, we do not conceal our conviction that perestroika in the Soviet Union is in accordance with the very essence of socialism and the justified needs of social progress." A short while later, after referring to the right of each Communist party to resolve its own country's problems, Gorbachev immediately qualified this with the stricture that each member of the socialist commonwealth must show "obligatory consideration not only for its own interests but also for common interests," echoing the Brezhnev Doctrine.[66]

Gorbachev's continued ambivalence about Soviet–East European relations was also reflected in his attempt during his visit to Czechoslovakia not to

---

[63] See, for example, "Wesentlicher Inhalt der Ausführungen des Ministers für Verteidigung der UdSSR, Genossen Marschall der Sowjetunion Sokolow, am 18 Mai 1987," Notes from Sokolov's Remarks to Warsaw Pact Defense Ministers, No. 1c\021\87 (Top Secret), May 18, 1987, in BA – Abt. MA, VA-01/40373, Bl. 124–128

[64] "Vstrecha Gorbacheva s sekretaryami TsK bratskikh partii po sel'skomu khozyaistvu, 11 fevryalya 1987 goda," Transcript of Discussion (Top Secret), February 11, 1987, transcribed in KDPP, Vol. 2, pp. 89–91.

[65] "Miting Chekhoslovatsko-sovetskoi druzhby: Rech' tovarishcha Gorbacheva M. S.," *Pravda* (Moscow), April 11, 1987, p. 2.

[66] Ibid.

mention, either favorably or unfavorably, the Soviet-led invasion of the country in August 1968. When confronted unexpectedly about the issue during a tour of Bratislava, he first tried to avoid a direct answer, describing the Prague Spring as a "stern school" and a "difficult period" that the Soviet Union and Czechoslovakia had "experienced together with dignity and honor." But then, to the surprise of many who had come to hear his "new thinking," he suddenly added a blunt endorsement of the Soviet invasion: "We [in Moscow and Prague] have bravely thought about what happened.... We came to the right conclusions then. Look how far Czechoslovakia has advanced since 1968."[67]

The Warsaw Pact's New Military Doctrine

This uneasy combination of "old thinking" and "new thinking" set the stage for a high-level internal debate in Moscow in May 1987 that preceded the adoption of a new military doctrine for the Warsaw Pact. The main point of contention was not *whether* the Warsaw Pact should adopt a "defensive" doctrine – no one argued against this – but what exactly such a doctrine would mean in practice and what the state of the NATO–Warsaw Pact military balance was. At a CPSU Politburo meeting on May 7, Marshal Sergei Sokolov clashed with Foreign Minister Eduard Shevardnadze, who argued that the Soviet Union and its allies enjoyed considerable advantages in certain categories of weaponry and therefore had leeway to scale back their forces so that they would conform better with a defensive doctrine.[68] The implication was that modest, carefully chosen cuts of specific types of weapons would be beneficial, rather than detrimental, to Soviet security.

Interpreting Shevardnadze's remarks as a call for wide-ranging unilateral reductions of Soviet and East European weaponry, Sokolov insisted that any cuts in Warsaw Pact deployments must be reciprocated by NATO and that any unilateral moves would "disrupt the existing balance" and undermine the Soviet Union's "capacity to destroy our enemy in the event of an attack – a capacity we must preserve at all costs." The Warsaw Pact, he added, must be "ready for a nuclear war as well as for a war fought solely with conventional weapons." Alluding to Germany's devastating attack on the USSR in June 1941, Sokolov warned that the Soviet armed forces must never "yield territory to NATO aggressors. Every meter of ground of the socialist states must be defended."[69]

---

[67] "Obshchie tseli, edinyi kurs: Prebyvanie M. S. Gorbacheva v Slovakii," *Pravda* (Moscow), April 12, 1987, p. 1.

[68] "Zasedanie Politbyuro TsK KPSS 7 maya 1987 goda," Transcript, May 7, 1987 (Top Secret), in KDPP, Vol. 2, pp. 261–276.

[69] Ibid., pp. 267–269.

When the discussion continued without resolution, Gorbachev designated a smaller group headed by Lev Zaikov to coordinate suggestions for the new Warsaw Pact military doctrine and to consider whether to "publish accurate data about the disposition of [Soviet and East European] military forces in Central Europe."[70] The next day, debate about the proposed doctrine resumed in the full CPSU Politburo, though it soon became clear that Gorbachev had swung his support to Shevardnadze. Shevardnadze's predecessor, Andrei Gromyko, who was still a Politburo member and the head of state, contended that the military balance did not favor the Warsaw Pact and that any Soviet force reductions would be dangerous unless they were matched by at least equal cuts in NATO's weaponry. Gromyko evidently hoped that his stature as the foreign policy *eminence grise* on the Politburo would give greater weight to the objections voiced earlier by Sokolov, who was only a candidate member. Far from backing down, however, Gorbachev chided Gromyko, arguing that "a defensive military doctrine ... is not just an empty declaration of principles. It must also be a program for the development [and restructuring] of our armed forces."[71] The Politburo approved the adoption and implementation of a defensive military doctrine, but over the next few weeks, as the final version of the new doctrine was being prepared, Sokolov and other high-ranking Soviet military officers sought to ensure that the proclamation of a defensive posture would not require any appreciable change in Soviet–Warsaw Pact military deployments and practices, including the alliance's traditional emphasis on large-scale offensive operations against NATO.

These rearguard actions by military officers were, however, largely undercut by two factors, one of which was purely fortuitous. First and most important was the growing link in Gorbachev's mind between Soviet military policy and his domestic economic priorities. Funding for military activities and the defense industry had long absorbed an outsize share of the overall Soviet budget.[72] Gorbachev had been aware of this as a high-ranking party official since the late 1970s, and he learned more about the matter after he became General Secretary of the CPSU in March 1985. After he adopted a sweeping program of industrial modernization in the latter half of 1985, his

---

[70] Ibid., p. 275.
[71] "Zasedanie Politbyuro TsK KPSS 8 maya 1987 goda," Transcript, May 8, 1987 (Top Secret), in KDPP, Vol. 2, pp. 278–287.
[72] Mark Harrison, "Secrets, Lies, and Half Truths: The Decision to Disclose Soviet Defense Outlays," PERSA Working Paper No. 55 (Warwick: Political Economy Research in Soviet Archives, September 2008); Mark Harrison, "How Much Did the Soviets Really Spend on Defence? New Evidence from the Close of the Brezhnev Era," Warwick Economic Research Papers No. 662 (United Kingdom: University of Warwick, January 2003); and William Easterly and Stanley Fischer, "The Soviet Economic Decline," *The World Bank Economic Review*, Vol. 9, No. 3 (September 1995), pp. 341–371.

closest advisers warned him that the success of the program would depend in part on his ability to set a limit on the resources that would have to be committed to the Soviet armed forces over the next two to three decades.[73] Gorbachev's aides argued that even if he could not make immediate cuts in the defense budget, he would have to ensure that resource commitments to military programs over the longer term (i.e., starting with the Five-Year Plan in 1991) would be constrained and predictable. They told him that if the Soviet Union continued to allocate all its best resources, both human and material, to military industries at the expense of the nonmilitary industrial base, his efforts to promote economic restructuring and technological prowess would be jeopardized.

Hence, by 1986 Gorbachev was intent on defusing any pressures that might arise at home or abroad for a future military buildup. A reinvigoration of East–West arms control negotiations, which had been in abeyance since 1983 after the USSR walked out of talks on intermediate-range nuclear forces, was one crucial element of this strategy. At a Soviet Politburo meeting in mid-1986, Gorbachev described arms control agreements with NATO countries as a prerequisite for "reductions of [our] defense expenditures so that we can count on achieving an increase in living standards."[74]

Nonetheless, even if the East–West negotiations eventually proved fruitful (and there was no guarantee that they would), Gorbachev surmised at an early stage that arms control alone would be insufficient. He increasingly sensed that he would have to move away from the traditional Soviet style of force planning, which in the past had always been the exclusive preserve of high-ranking military officers on the Soviet General Staff, who were wont to operate on the basis of worst-case scenarios and inflated threat assessments. Gorbachev did not seek to displace the General Staff as a source of advice, but he deliberately cultivated alternatives outside the armed forces in a bid to generate innovative ideas. In particular, he consulted civilian experts at the Soviet Foreign Ministry, the CPSU International Department, and various Soviet Academy of Sciences institutes, who could provide a different conception of national security and Soviet national interests.[75] The idea of formulating a defensive military doctrine for the Warsaw Pact originated not with the General Staff but with these new civilian advisers, who produced a draft that was then modified by the General Staff. In early May 1987, the Soviet draft was presented to the defense ministers

---

[73] Chernyaev, *Shest' let s Gorbachevym*, pp. 55–56, 115.
[74] "Zasedanie Politbyuro TsK KPSS 13 iyunya 1986 goda," Transcript, June 13, 1986 (Top Secret), in KDPP, Vol. 1, p. 123.
[75] Mark Kramer, "The Role of the CPSU International Department in Soviet Foreign Relations and National Security Policy," *Soviet Studies*, Vol. 42, No. 2 (July 1990), pp. 429–447.

of all the other Warsaw Pact countries, who put together an expert group to coordinate a final draft. Despite some minor revisions introduced by the East Germans and more significant changes proposed by the Romanians, the final statement was largely identical to the original Soviet draft – an outcome that often happened when Soviet drafts were presented as faits accomplis.[76]

The public enunciation of the Warsaw Pact's new doctrine at a key meeting of its PCC on May 29, 1987 had obvious propaganda benefits for the USSR and the alliance as a whole, but that was by no means the only purpose of the declaration.[77] Gorbachev and his aides believed the time had come to launch a fundamental restructuring of the Warsaw Pact.

Any such restructuring, of course, could not be achieved in a day or even a year. The goal instead was to initiate the process and establish a predictable long-term framework for deploying much lower levels of force. This would give Gorbachev the type of stable climate in which he would be able to curb Soviet defense spending for a prolonged period and focus his attention on economic revitalization. The overriding importance of economic reform for Gorbachev helps to explain why he was willing to deflect the objections voiced by many Soviet military officers, who were averse to a far-reaching reorientation of the Warsaw Pact and wanted to preserve as much as possible of the alliance's capacity for large-scale offensive operations. Although Gorbachev privately assured Soviet military commanders that the new doctrine would not endanger Soviet interests, he stressed it was time to "show that our words about defensive postures are matched in deeds."[78]

The long-standing tradition of civilian control over the Soviet armed forces ensured that Soviet military officers would go along with the proposed changes in the Warsaw Pact. Their compliance, however, was grudging at best. Sokolov, Kulikov, and other commanders were still privately convinced that a full-scale shift to a defensive orientation and a renunciation of preemptive options would

---

[76] On the behind-the-scenes drafting process, see "Generalsekretär des Zentralkomitees der Sozialistischen Einheitspartei Deutschlands und Vorsitzenden des Nationalen Verteidigungsrates der Deutschen Demokratischen Republik, Genossen Erich Honecker," Memorandum No. A-138/87 (Secret) from Army-General Heinz Keßler, East German national defense minister, to SED General Seretary Erich Honecker, May 27, 1987, in SAPMO-BA, DC20/I/3/2477, Ss. 44–47. The Romanian proposals, which were debated but not incorporated, were presented by Keßler to Honecker in a one-page appendix ("Anlage: Wesentlichste Forderungen der Vertreter der Sozialistische Republik Rumänien"), S. 48.

[77] "O voennoi doktrine gosudarstv-uchastnikov Varshavskogo Dogovora," *Krasnaya zvezda* (Moscow), May 30, 1987, p. 1.

[78] "Anlage 2: Wesentlicher Inhalt der Ausführungen des Generalsekretärs des Zentralkomitees der KPdSU, Genossen Michail Gorbatschow, wahrend des Treffens mit den Mitgliedern des Komitees der Verteidigungsminister am 07. 07. 1988," Verbatim Transcript of Gorbachev's Remarks to Warsaw Pact Defense Ministers (Top Secret), July 7, 1988, in BA – Abt. MA, DVW 1/71049, Bl. 6–13.

erode Soviet security and "allow the aggressor [i.e., NATO] to enjoy a military-strategic advantage."[79] Nonetheless, the officers' ability to mitigate the impact of the new doctrine was hindered by a second factor – a factor that no one could have expected. On May 28, 1987, as the PCC meeting was under way, a young West German citizen named Mathias Rust piloted a Cessna-172 sports plane on an unauthorized flight from Finland deep into the Soviet Union and eventually landed on a bridge alongside Red Square in Moscow, much to the amazement of passersby and police officers.[80] This bizarre incident drew worldwide attention and had momentous consequences for the Soviet High Command. Two days after Rust's incursion, Defense Minister Sokolov resigned under pressure, and the commander-in-chief of the Soviet Air Defense Forces was dismissed. In subsequent weeks, many other high-ranking military officers were also removed, marking the largest turnover of Soviet Defense Ministry personnel in several decades.

Gorbachev, who was enraged and deeply unnerved by the incident, was able to use it to tighten his hold over the armed forces and to accelerate the downgrading of the military's ceremonial role.[81] In the age of *glasnost* the Rust affair was discussed extensively in the Soviet media, and the tone of the coverage was overwhelmingly negative about the Soviet High Command. Much of the criticism was targeted at genuine shortcomings and abuses, especially problems in training, combat initiative, and airfield security. Some of the commentaries, however, amounted to little more than a string of insults, accusing military officers of "rudeness, boorishness, and intimidation" and of engendering a climate conducive to "toadies, boot-lickers, sycophants, and window-dressers."[82] In retrospect, these charges may seem excessive, but at the time they reflected the sentiments of many Soviet citizens, who had been told for decades that their country's airspace was inviolable and that Soviet troops would "rebuff any attempts to breach our country's security or to encroach on our borders." Gorbachev typified the public mood at a CPSU Politburo meeting on May 30 when he described the incident as an "unprecedented humiliation" that was "indicative of the general situation in the Armed Forces."[83] The resulting

---

[79] Comments of Marshal Kulikov, transcribed in "Wichtigster Inhalt der Beratung der Chefs der General-(Haupt-) stabe in Moskau," October 14, 1987, in BA – Abt. MA, VA-01/32659, Bl. 68.
[80] For a detailed account of the Rust affair and its impact, see Mark Kramer, "Air Defense Forces," in David R. Jones, ed., *Soviet Armed Forces Review Annual 1987–88* (Gulf Breeze, FL: Academic International Press, 1989), pp. 105–162, esp. 112–122.
[81] Chernyaev, *Shest' let s Gorbachevym*, pp. 156–161.
[82] Colonel B. Pokholenchuk and Lieutenant-Colonel V. Gavrilenko, "Po zakonam vysokoi otvetsvennosti: Sobraniya partiinogo aktiva Moskovskogo okruga PVO,"*Krasnaya zvezda* (Moscow), June 17, 1987, p. 2.
[83] "Zasedanie Politbyuro TsK KPSS 30 maya 1987 goda," Transcript, May 30, 1987 (Top Secret), in KDPP, Vol. 2, pp. 327–328. See also "Zasedanie Politbyuro TsK KPSS 4 iyunya 1987 goda," Transcript, June 4, 1987 (Top Secret), in KDPP, Vol. 2, pp. 328–329.

diminution of the military's political clout in the wake of the Rust affair was striking. Until May 1987, *glasnost* had extended only tentatively into discussions of the Soviet Army, but Rust's intrusion into Moscow clearly struck a raw nerve and dispelled the aura that had long surrounded the army.

The fallout from the Rust affair not only facilitated Gorbachev's efforts to move ahead with arms control (notably the Intermediate-Range Nuclear Forces Treaty) but also made it more difficult for senior military officers to thwart or hinder the implementation of the Warsaw Pact's new doctrine. With the spread of *glasnost* into the military sphere, efforts to obstruct the doctrine were more apt to come to public light. As a result, Soviet commanders drafted concrete proposals to restructure the Soviet and East European armed forces and to revise the alliance's operational plans. These initiatives laid the groundwork for a far-reaching reconfiguration of the Pact. The new Soviet defense minister, Army-General Dmitrii Yazov, whom Gorbachev had elevated over several higher-ranking officers, was no more enthusiastic about the Warsaw Pact's military doctrine than other Soviet commanders were. But Yazov realized that in his initial months in office, he could not give the impression that he was already trying to weaken or circumvent the doctrine.[84]

Yet even as serious planning and preparations began in the military sphere to alter the Warsaw Pact, Gorbachev had not yet decided how far he was willing to go with broader changes in Soviet–East European political and military relations. In his keynote speech in November 1987 marking the 70th anniversary of the Bolsheviks' rise to power, he spoke briefly about Eastern Europe, declaring that "all [Communist] parties are fully and irreversibly independent. We said this as far back as the 20th [Party] Congress. True, it took time to free ourselves from old habits. Now, however, it is an immutable reality."[85] But a few minutes later Gorbachev sharply narrowed the latitude for independent action by stipulating that relations among Soviet-bloc countries must be based on "the practice of socialist internationalism," including a "concern for the general cause of socialism" – echoing phrases that were used in 1968 to justify the invasion of Czechoslovakia. He then added an even more explicit restatement of key parts of the Brezhnev Doctrine: "We know what damage can be caused by weakening the internationalist principle in the mutual relations of socialist states, by

---

[84] Dmitrii Yazov, *Udary sud'by: Vospominaniya soldata i marshala* (Moscow: Kniga i biznes, 2002), pp. 359–360.

[85] "Oktyabr' i perestroika: Revolyutsiya prodolzhaetsya – Doklad General'nogo sekretarya TsK KPSS M. S. Gorbacheva," *Pravda* (Moscow), November 3, 1987, p. 5. In the weeks prior to Gorbachev's speech, the CPSU Politburo discussed various drafts in great detail, but the often heated debate focused almost exclusively on how to reassess and present the darker periods of Soviet history. The sections on foreign policy, including Eastern Europe, did not spark any controversy.

deviating from the principles of mutual benefit and mutual assistance, and by neglecting to heed the common interests of socialism in action on the world scene."[86]

A similar message was conveyed in Gorbachev's book *Perestroika*, which was published in both East and West just after the 70th anniversary celebrations of 1917 (Gorbachev had worked extensively on it during a break in the late summer). The book acknowledged certain shortcomings in Soviet relations with East European countries in the past, and it pledged that every Communist state would have full independence to proceed along its own path of development. But the brief section on Eastern Europe went no further than Gorbachev's earlier statements, and it contained a key passage that linked the domestic complexion of each member of the socialist commonwealth with the interests of all others:

> The socialist community will be successful only if every party and state cares for both its own interests and common interests, if it respects its friends and allies, heeds their interests, and pays attention to the experience of others. Awareness of this relationship between domestic issues and the interests of world socialism is typical of the countries of the socialist community. We are united, in unity resides our strength.[87]

For East European readers of the book, this assertion of a "relationship between domestic issues and the interests of world socialism" was all too evocative of the Brezhnev Doctrine. In no respect did the book imply that drastic change in the political systems of Eastern Europe and a curtailment of Soviet hegemony would ever be tolerable. The continued uncertainty about the leeway for political change in the Soviet bloc provided the backdrop for the proposed overhaul of the Warsaw Pact.

Restructuring and Reductions of Forces

By the end of 1987, as General Yazov got acclimated to his new post at the Defense Ministry, he joined Marshal Kulikov and other high-ranking officers in trying to circumscribe the concrete impact of the Warsaw Pact's new military doctrine. Kulikov repeatedly insisted, both privately and publicly, that the Soviet and East European armed forces would have to maintain "the ability not only to repulse aggression but also to destroy the opponent through resolute offensive operations."[88] He warned that the Warsaw Pact countries could "not risk any reduction in military expenditures" or any "relaxation of our vigilance"

---

[86] Ibid.

[87] Mikhail Gorbachev, *Perestroika: New Thinking for Our Country and the World* (New York: Harper and Row, 1987), p. 165.

[88] Comments transcribed in "Wichtigster Inhalt der Beratung der Chefs der General-(Haupt-) stabe in Moskau," Bl. 69.

against the West. Yazov, for his part, castigated "pacifists" who engaged in "wishful thinking" about reducing the size of the joint armed forces while also maintaining parity with NATO.[89] Many Soviet commanders were uneasy about the precedent set by the Intermediate-Range Nuclear Forces (INF) Treaty signed in December 1987, which imposed heavier obligations on the USSR than on the United States in the number of nuclear missiles eliminated and which came to fruition only after far-reaching Soviet concessions excluding British and French missiles from the treaty's limits. High-ranking Soviet officers worried that Gorbachev might soon heed the advice of civilian officials who were calling for unilateral reductions of Soviet conventional forces deployed in Eastern Europe, including frontline units arrayed against NATO.[90] The rationale for such cuts was that they would facilitate a mutual scaling-back of the East–West confrontation in Europe, but Soviet military commanders feared that NATO either would decline to reciprocate or would make only cosmetic moves of its own.

The renewed foot-dragging by senior military personnel prompted reform-minded civilian officials to urge Gorbachev to intervene. In late May 1988, Shakhnazarov, who by then had moved over to Gorbachev's personal staff as a senior adviser on foreign and domestic issues, sent a memorandum to Gorbachev expressing concern about a report drafted by Marshal Kulikov for a meeting of the PCC that was slated to be held in mid-July.[91] Shakhnazarov averred that Kulikov's report "gives the impression that despite our repeated assurances about our embrace of a defensive military doctrine, we have not actually even begun to think about the strategic concepts needed to achieve it." He condemned Kulikov's "flimsy" and "unconvincing" assertion that "even with the signing of the INF Treaty, the military danger in Europe, far from diminishing, is actually growing." Shakhnazarov argued that Kulikov's proposals would require a "sharp increase in military expenditures" that would push both the Soviet Union and the East European countries "into economic collapse." He said that key parts of the report were "incomprehensible" and that Kulikov was "construing the notion of a defensive doctrine in a very fanciful way." Not only had the marshal called for

---

[89] "Wesentlicher Inhalt der Ausführungen des Ministers für Verteidigung der UdSSR: Genossen Armeegeneral Jasow, auf der Beratung zu Fragen der militärisch-technischen Seite der Militärdoktrin der Teilnehmerstaaten des Warschauer Vertrages am 26. 11. 1987," VVS-Nr. A 471 238 (Top Secret), November 26, 1987, in BA – Abt. MA, VA-32651, Bl. 5–6.

[90] See the comments of Marshal Sergei Akhromeev, then chief of the Soviet General Staff, in "Niederschrift über eine Beratung mit dem Ersten Stellvertreter des Ministers für Verteidigung der UdSSR und Chef des Generalstabes der Streitkräfte, Genossen Marschall der Sowjetunion Achromejew," March 15, 1988, in BA – Abt. MA, VA-01/32660, Bl. 114–117.

[91] "K dokladu V. G. Kulikova na Soveshchanii PKK Varshavskogo Dogovora," May 25, 1988, Memorandum from Shakhnazarov to Gorbachev, in Arkhiv Gorbachev-Fonda (AGF), F. 5, Op. 1, Dok. 10747, Ll. 1–4.

a "large buildup of airborne forces," which "perform missions that are predominantly offensive," but he had also proposed to "strengthen chemical warfare forces," a move that would "cast obvious doubt on the sincerity of our support for the complete prohibition and elimination of chemical weapons." Shakhnazarov concluded that "overall what [Kulikov] is discussing here is not a reduction of military forces, but, on the contrary, a major increase of those forces." Western governments, he warned, "will naturally deduce that, regardless of what we say, we in fact are opposed not only to disarmament but also to any genuine diminution of the military confrontation."

Gorbachev read the memorandum closely and made extensive notations on it before sending "instructions" about the matter to Yazov, who ordered Kulikov to redraft the report. This episode set the tone for Gorbachev's speech at a session of the Warsaw Pact Council of Defense Ministers on July 7, 1988, a week before the PCC meeting. Using a text drafted mainly by Shakhnazarov with some input from the Soviet Defense Ministry, Gorbachev told the defense ministers that the USSR's "own security and the security of our allies ... depend less on purely military factors than on political, economic, and social conditions."[92] He argued that this "new understanding of allied security" should lead to a different conception of "parity" between East and West:

> We are accustomed to thinking in terms of parity. . . . But to some extent we have succumbed to a false logic of parity, which demands a balance of forces in every type of weaponry and in every possible theater of military operations. Having set out on this path, we have dragged ourselves into an endless, intractable arms race, giving in to the intrigues of the enemies of socialism. And in a more general sense we have even weakened our security. We cannot allow this to continue, not only because our economic potential does not permit it, but also because we do not believe that differences of social systems are pushing us toward a global military conflict. . . . Instead of a balance of forces we need a balance of interests. Instead of military parity we need parity of security.[93]

Gorbachev then explained how the redefined principles of security and parity would affect "the nature of the defensive military doctrine declared by us jointly last year in Berlin." He started out using language proposed by the Soviet Defense Ministry that Shakhnazarov had incorporated into his own draft of the speech:

---

[92] See the handwritten notes from the meeting on July 6–8, 1988, transcribed by Georgii Shakhnazarov, in AGF, F. 5, Op. 1, Dok. 10752, Ll. 1–14. Quotations from Gorbachev's speech are taken from these notes, with some fleshing out from the draft prepared by Shakhnazarov, "Material k vstreche s voennymi," July 6, 1988, in AGF, F. 5, Op. 1, Dok. 10570, Ll. 1–9, along with a cover note dated July 6, 1988. Gorbachev's mark-ups on the draft reflect how he couched it for his delivery.
[93] Ibid., L. 4.

The Fate of the Soviet Bloc's Military Alliance 31

> It is important to bring the whole structure of our armed forces into line with this doctrine and to eliminate the elements that do not fully correspond to it. This is a complicated, large-scale task. You, as military leaders, need to think about how to instill these fundamental propositions into the practice of structuring armed forces now and in the coming five-year period.[94]

But Gorbachev omitted the Defense Ministry's suggested phrasing about the need to "maintain [the Warsaw Pact's] armed forces and weapons at a level ensuring that any attack by an aggressor will not catch us off-guard."[95] Instead, the Soviet leader used Shakhnazarov's wording to underscore the significance he attached to the defensive doctrine:

> What is especially important here is to ensure that words match deeds and that socialism presents its true, peaceful, and constructive image rather than an image associated with reliance on weapons, fueled by the aggressive designs of the so-called "Eastern bear," as our enemies in the West like to call us. . . . The new circumstances also envisage a definite transformation of our views concerning NATO. Yes, we see the threat posed by this military bloc. But we also see a partner in negotiations aimed at reductions of weapons.[96]

Gorbachev reiterated many of the same themes in a lengthy speech at the PCC meeting a week later, exhorting the allied governments to do whatever they could to facilitate progress in arms control talks that would lead to simultaneous reductions of Warsaw Pact and NATO conventional forces, especially weapons most suited for offensive operations. He expanded on these points at a follow-up PCC meeting on August 5–6, 1987, which reaffirmed "defense sufficiency" as a cardinal tenet of the alliance and called for vigorous efforts to achieve reciprocal cuts in NATO and Warsaw Pact arsenals. But when the arms control negotiations bogged down and reached an impasse, Gorbachev shifted to unilateral reductions, an approach long dreaded by Soviet military officers. In a landmark speech at the United Nations (UN) General Assembly in December 1988, Gorbachev announced that the Soviet Union would unilaterally cut its military forces in Eastern Europe by 50,000 troops, 5,300 tanks, and 24 tactical nuclear weapons within two years.[97]

---

[94] Ibid.
[95] See "Material dlya besedy General'nogo sekretarya TsK KPSS M. S. Gorbacheva s chlenami Komiteta Ministerstv oborony (8 iyulya 1988 g.)," notes prepared by the Soviet Defense Ministry, July 5, 1988, in AGF, F. 5, Op. 1, Dok. 10751, Ll. 1–6. Shakhnazarov incorporated a few passages into his own draft (which was then used by Gorbachev), but he discarded most of what the ministry sent over after passing it on to Gorbachev.
[96] "Material k vstreche s voennymi," L. 4.
[97] "Vystuplenie M. S. Gorbacheva v Organizatsii Ob"edinennykh Natsii," *Pravda* (Moscow), December 8,1988, p. 2. The U.S. intelligence community in 1989 prepared several classified assessments of the military impact of these cuts. See, for example, U.S. Central Intelligence Agency (CIA), "Trends and Development in Warsaw Pact Theater Forces and Doctrine Through

The decision to reduce Soviet troops and weapons unilaterally, and the related decision about precisely which forces to eliminate, were made exclusively in Moscow. Initially, at the end of October 1988, Gorbachev met with a small group of foreign policy advisers, including Shevardnadze, Aleksandr Yakovlev, Anatolii Chernyaev, Anatolii Dobrynin, and Valentin Falin, to determine how the initiative should be formulated and presented.[98] The proposal was then fleshed out with specific numbers and discussed by the full CPSU Politburo on November 10 and 24, and December 2.[99] The USSR Defense Council, a high-level political-military body that Gorbachev also chaired, met on November 11 to determine which Soviet forces should be weeded out and how quickly they should be withdrawn. In none of these deliberations did the East European leaders have any say or play even the slightest role. Last-minute "consultations" with the East European governments about the matter, after key decisions had already been made, were purely pro forma. The East German leader Erich Honecker, whose country was the most heavily affected by the reductions, was informed of Gorbachev's intentions only three days before the Soviet leader spoke at the UN.[100] According to Honecker's former associates, he was "stunned and dismayed" by the news, but he had little choice other than to express his perfunctory endorsement and to avoid any comments that would betray his unhappiness about the forthcoming cuts.[101]

The aim of the reductions, according to the resolution adopted by the CPSU Politburo, was to "accentuate the defensive character" of the Warsaw Pact, to "give new, powerful momentum to the process of lowering the military-strategic

---

the 1990s," National Intelligence Estimate (NIE) 11–14–89 (Top Secret), February 1989, reproduced in CIA, Center for the Study of Intelligence, *At Cold War's End: U.S. Intelligence on the Soviet Union and Eastern Europe, 1989–1991* (Washington, DC: CIA 1999), Document 16. See also Odom, *The Collapse of the Soviet Military*, pp. 146–147.

[98] "Soveshchanie po podgotovke kontseptsii vystupleniya Gorbacheva v OON," notes taken by Anatolii Chernyaev, October 31, 1988, in KDPP, Vol. 3, pp. 491–494.

[99] "Zasedanie Politbyuro TsK KPSS 10 noyabrya 1988 goda," Transcript, November 10, 1988 (Top Secret), in KDPP, Vol. 3, pp. 498–509; "Zasedanie Politbyuro TsK KPSS 24 noyabrya 1988 goda," Transcript, November 24, 1988 (Top Secret), in KDPP, Vol. 3, pp. 509–522; and "Zasedanie Politbyuro TsK KPSS 10 dekabrya 1988 goda," Transcript, December 2, 1988 (Top Secret), in KDPP, Vol. 3, pp. 524–529.

[100] "Wesentlicher Inhalt des Gesprächs des Generalsekretärs des ZK der SED und Vorsitzenden des Nationalen Verteiddigungsrates der DDR, Genossen Erich Honecker, mit dem Mitglied des Politbüros des ZK der SED und Minister für Nationale Verteidigung, Genossen Armeegeneral Keßler, am Sonntag, dem or. 12. 1988," GVS-Nr. A 613 225 (Top Secret), December 4, 1988, in BA – Abt. MA, VA-01/32665, Bl. 154–160.

[101] See, for example, the comments of Heinz Keßler, *Zur Sache und zur Person: Erinnerungen* (Berlin: Edition Ost, 1996), pp. 240–241; Hans Modrow, *Aufbruch und Ende* (Hamburg: Konkret Literatur, 1991), p. 131; Hans Modrow, *In historischer Mission: als deutscher Politiker unterwegs* (Berlin: Edition Ost, 2007), p. 181; Egon Krenz, *Herbst '89* (Berlin: Neues Leben, 1999), p. 107; and Egon Krenz, *Wenn Mauern fallen: Die friedliche Revolution – Vorgeschichte, Ablauf-Auswirkungen* (Vienna: Paul Neff, 1990), pp. 23–24.

balance in Europe," and to "improve relations between East and West and facilitate the process of disarmament."[102] This last point was especially important for Gorbachev, who viewed the unilateral cuts as the best way to achieve economic savings in the near to medium term and to foster stability for the future. At a CPSU Politburo meeting a few weeks after the speech, he claimed that unless the Soviet Union reduced its military forces and defense spending, it would "never be able to sustain a longer-term economic and social policy."[103]

In both military and political terms, the reductions amply fulfilled Gorbachev's objectives. The U.S. intelligence community, which carefully tracked the implementation of Gorbachev's projected cuts, reported in September 1989 that the withdrawals were leading to "a very significant reduction in the offensive combat power of Soviet forces in Europe" and would "produce over the next few years the most significant changes in Soviet general-purpose forces opposite NATO since [Nikita] Khrushchev's drastic force reductions of the late 1950s and early 1960s." U.S. intelligence analysts concluded that even if the Soviet Army added infantry fighting vehicles and armored personnel carriers to its units in Eastern Europe to make up for the cuts, "the loss of half the [Soviet] tanks previously stationed in Eastern Europe will significantly degrade Pact offensive capabilities."[104] From a political standpoint as well, the impact of the reductions was enormous. Gorbachev assured the Soviet Politburo that the cuts would "show that our new political thinking is more than just words" and would signal a new Soviet approach to relations with Eastern Europe. Some members of the Soviet Politburo warned that the reductions, by strengthening the impression that the Soviet Union would no longer provide "fraternal assistance" to the East European regimes, might entail "undesirable consequences for the entire socialist commonwealth."[105] But Gorbachev was willing to accept that risk as he pressed ahead with his efforts to revive and restructure the Soviet economy, to recast Soviet foreign relations in accordance with his "new political thinking," and to transform the Warsaw Pact into a defensive alliance.

The decision to embrace unilateral reductions along with the new military doctrine provoked consternation within the Soviet High Command. The very

---

[102] "Wesentlicher Inhalt des Gesprächs des Generalsekretärs des ZK der SED und Vorsitzenden des Nationalen Verteiddigungsrates der DDR, Genossen Erich Honecker, mit dem Mitglied des Politbüros des ZK der SED und Minister für Nationale Verteidigung, Genossen Armeegeneral Keßler," Bl. 158.

[103] "Zasedanie Politbyuro TsK KPSS 27–28 dekabrya 1988 goda: O prakticheskoi realizatsii i prakticheskom obespechenii itogov vizita t. Gorbacheva M. S. v OON," Transcript, December 27–28, 1988 (Top Secret), in RGANI, F. 89, Op. 42, D. 24, Ll. 1–34.

[104] U.S. National Intelligence Council, "Status of Soviet Unilateral Withdrawals," Memorandum NIC M 89 10003 (Secret), October 1989, pp. 2, 8, reproduced in CSI, *At Cold War's End*, Doc. 18.

[105] "Zasedanie Politbyuro TsK KPSS 27–28 dekabrya 1988 goda," L. 31.

thing that Soviet marshals and generals had long been denouncing as a "dangerous," "misguided," and "completely unacceptable" option was now enshrined as state policy. The chief of the Soviet General Staff, Marshal Sergei Akhromeev, resigned five days before Gorbachev's speech at the UN. Although Akhromeev at the time did not publicly disclose why he stepped down, and although he agreed to stay on temporarily as a personal military adviser to Gorbachev, he later revealed that he had been "stunned" and "distraught" over Gorbachev's willingness to act without gaining reciprocity by NATO.[106] In Akhromeev's view, this was "incomprehensible" and a "betrayal." In subsequent weeks, many other high-ranking Soviet officers were dismissed, climaxing with the replacement of Marshal Kulikov and his chief deputy, Army-General Anatolii Gribkov, in early February 1989. The ouster of Kulikov and Gribkov, who had been serving together in the two highest command positions of the Warsaw Pact since 1977, brought a symbolic end to the Soviet Army's attempts to preserve the Pact as a cohesive, potent alliance. From then on, Soviet military officers were hoping mainly that they could salvage key components of the organization and stave off outright collapse.

Reorientation of Soviet Policy

Gorbachev's shift to a much bolder approach vis-à-vis the Warsaw Pact in 1988, with his embrace of unilateral reductions and the restructuring of Soviet forces, coincided with a more general reorientation of his policy toward Eastern Europe. When he visited Yugoslavia in March 1988, he signed a joint communiqué pledging "unconditional" respect for "the principles of equality and non-interference" and for "the independence of parties and socialist countries to define, for themselves, the path of their own development."[107] Although most of the communiqué applied specifically to Soviet–Yugoslav relations amid growing ferment in post-Tito Yugoslavia, the phrases about independence, equality, and noninterference referred to the whole of the Soviet bloc.

Gorbachev soon made good on these pledges by giving the East European countries much greater latitude for internal political liberalization and market-oriented economic reform – latitude that Hungary and Poland (though not the four other countries) were quick to exploit. Moreover, for the first time, Soviet analysts began to reevaluate and criticize the whole postwar history of Soviet–East European relations. As early as May 1988 a lengthy article in an influential publication, the weekly *Literaturnaya gazeta*, by the prominent "new thinker"

---

[106] Interview with Akhromeev in "Deutschland, das neue Europa, und die Perestroika: Exklusivinterview mit Marschall Achromejev," *Neues Deutschland* (Berlin), October 4, 1990, p. 8.

[107] "Sovetsko-yugoslavskaya deklaratsiya," *Pravda* (Moscow), March 19, 1988, p. 1.

The Fate of the Soviet Bloc's Military Alliance 35

Vyacheslav Dashichev stressed that the Soviet Union's "hegemonic policies and great-power mentality" in Eastern Europe after 1945, as reflected in "the spread of Stalinist socialism wherever possible and its standardization in all countries regardless of their national features," had been directly responsible for the cycle of "sharp confrontations and armed clashes between socialist countries."[108] Dashichev condemned "the expulsion of Yugoslavia from the socialist system in 1948 and the attribution of all deadly sins to its leaders for the simple reason that they had refused to submit to [Joseph] Stalin and obey his dictates." Dashichev was equally scathing about the "mistakes and incompetence" of other Soviet leaders, especially Brezhnev, vis-à-vis Eastern Europe. By the latter half of 1988, criticisms of this sort were appearing regularly in the Soviet press.

The main elements of Dashichev's critique were incorporated into a "discussion paper" compiled in mid-1988 by the Institute of Economics of the World Socialist System (IEMSS), the only research institute in the Soviet Academy of Sciences that dealt primarily with Eastern Europe and intra-bloc ties. The authors of the paper called for drastic changes in Soviet–East European relations to overcome the "stagnant neo-Stalinism" bred by the "hegemonic aspirations" of earlier Soviet leaders.[109] Although the IEMSS did not have a direct role in the USSR's policymaking process, the institute was an important source of advice and information for senior officials in the CPSU and the Soviet government. The IEMSS director, Oleg Bogomolov, often conferred with some of Gorbachev's most influential aides, including Aleksandr Yakovlev and Georgii Shakhnazarov. By disseminating the paper to policymakers and by publishing it in Moscow and abroad, the IEMSS helped to make Soviet officials aware of the volatile conditions in East-Central Europe.

Gorbachev himself received a draft of the IEMSS paper from Shakhnazarov in June 1988 amid preparations for the CPSU's 19th Party Conference and for important meetings of the Warsaw Pact's military-political bodies.[110] A cover note from Shakhnazarov summarizing the document was marked by Gorbachev in various places, indicating that he had read it (and presumably had also read the attached full draft). When the Soviet leader delivered his keynote speech at the CPSU's 19th Conference in late June 1988, he echoed many points in the IEMSS

---

[108] Vyacheslav Dashichev, "Vostok-zapad: poisk novykh otnoshenii – O prioritetakh vneshnei politiki Sovetskogo gosudarstva," *Literaturnaya gazeta* (Moscow), No. 20 (May 18, 1988), p. 14. In December 1988, Dashichev's article was voted one of the best to have appeared in *Literaturnaya gazeta* in 1988.

[109] The paper was published in both Moscow and the West. See "East-West Relations and Eastern Europe: The Soviet Perspective," *Problems of Communism*, Vol. 37, No. 3 (May-August 1988), pp. 60–67.

[110] Memorandum from Shakhnazarov to Gorbachev, June 11, 1988, with draft of IEMSS paper attached, in AGF, F. 1, Op. 1, Dok. 11731.

document. Eschewing the platitudes used at earlier Soviet party and state gatherings, he condemned "the sediment that has accumulated on our relations" with the East European countries and promised that the Soviet Union in the future would adhere to a much different policy: "The external imposition of a social system, of a way of life, or of policies by any means, let alone military, is a dangerous trapping of the past."[111] In subsequent months, Gorbachev returned to this theme many times, both publicly and privately. In February 1989, for example, when he met with party and state officials in Soviet Ukraine, he told them that the USSR was "restructuring its relations with the socialist countries" and would henceforth be emphasizing their rights to "unconditional independence, full equality, strict non-interference in internal affairs, and rectification of the many deformities and mistakes linked with earlier periods in the history of socialism."[112]

Gorbachev's remarks in Ukraine came a few weeks after he had appointed General Petr Lushev as the new commander-in-chief of the Warsaw Pact, but neither Lushev nor his new deputies initially seemed to grasp the profound changes that were beginning to transform the alliance. When preparations got under way at the Soviet Ministry of Defense in the first few months of 1989 for planned celebrations in May 1990 of the 35th anniversary of the formation of the Warsaw Pact, the posters, banners, pamphlets, and other items that emanated from the ministry reflected orthodox conceptions of the Pact's role as a Soviet-dominated alliance committed to the preservation of Communist regimes. All the materials for the forthcoming anniversary could just as easily have been produced a decade earlier for the 25th anniversary (see Figure 1). By the time the 35th anniversary came around in May 1990, the items prepared a year earlier seemed like quaint relics of a bygone era.

The Secret Reinterpretation of Soviet Obligations under the Warsaw Pact

The fate of the Warsaw Pact was markedly affected by Gorbachev's ever greater willingness to jettison long-standing Soviet policies toward Eastern Europe. In the first few months of 1989, at his behest, the CPSU Politburo and Soviet Defense Council endorsed crucial guidelines about how the Soviet Union should respond to possible internal upheavals in Eastern Europe.[113] In effect, Gorbachev persuaded the members of the Politburo and Defense Council to join him in

---

[111] "Doklad General'nogo sekretarya TsK KPSS M. S. Gorbacheva na XIX Vsesoyuznoi konferentsii KPSS 28 iyunya 1988 goda," *Pravda* (Moscow), June 29, 1988, p. 3.

[112] "Rech' M. S. Gorbacheva na vstreche s trudyashchimisya v g. Kieve," *Krasnaya zvezda* (Moscow), February 24, 1989, p. 3.

[113] This section draws in part on material from Kramer, "The Demise of the Soviet Bloc," pp. 788–854.

Figure 1 This official Soviet poster, printed in Moscow in 1989, looks ahead to celebrations of the 35th anniversary of the formation of the Warsaw Pact planned for 1990. The poster shows the flags of the seven allied countries along with seven main battle tanks on parade. The caption in Russian reads "Together We Are Invincible." The shield at the top right reads "The Warsaw Pact is 35 Years Old." By the time the 35th anniversary actually came around in May 1990, this poster was nowhere on display.

deciding well in advance that the Soviet Union would not take military action in Eastern Europe, even if the Communist governments there collapsed. Gorbachev thus ensured that his colleagues on the Politburo and Defense Council – the only people who potentially could get rid of him – bore equal responsibility for this momentous decision and had no basis for moving against him if he declined to authorize military repression in the face of widespread destabilizing unrest in Eastern Europe. By forging a high-level consensus in Moscow as events gathered pace in Eastern Europe, Gorbachev sought to avoid being placed in an untenable situation if East European Communist regimes encountered popular turmoil and urged the Soviet Union to intervene on their behalf.

The process began on January 24, 1989 when Gorbachev received a memorandum from one of his top aides, Vadim Zagladin, who said he wanted to "draw [the Soviet leader's] attention to a very delicate and complicated matter that could take on immense significance for us."[114] Zagladin averred that the Soviet Union's "new military-political thinking" necessitated a "painstaking review of our obligations regarding the provision of military assistance to foreign states in extreme circumstances." The phrase "extreme circumstances" (*chrezvychainye obstoyatel'stva*), which could also be translated as "an emergency" in English, clearly referred not only to an external military attack by NATO (which was deemed unlikely by this time) but also to a severe internal crisis, including the downfall of the Communist regime. Zagladin warned that as long as the Soviet Union's existing obligations remained intact, "extreme circumstances might compel us to take actions that could halt and even totally negate what we have achieved" through the embrace of "new political thinking." He argued that "obligations undertaken amid the circumstances of the Cold War ... have sharply constrained [the Soviet Union's] freedom of action," and he expressed particular anxiety about "unpublished and, for the most part, tightly held documents regarding certain understandings that could potentially create severe difficulties for us." Zagladin said that in the future the Soviet Union must always "approach this issue from the perspective of new military-political thinking," which presumably would bring the elimination of "outdated commitments" to protect hardline regimes. In his view, the best way to "begin [is] by thoroughly analyzing *all* obligations we have undertaken that involve military assistance of any sort."[115]

Gorbachev promptly authorized Zagladin to coordinate an in-depth, high-level review of the matter that would offer recommendations for the CPSU Politburo. On January 27, Zagladin sent a note to senior officials responsible for foreign

---

[114] "Dokladnaya zapiska o peresmotre obyazatel'stv po okazaniyu voennoi pomoshchi," Memorandum from V. Zagladin to Mikhail Gorbachev (Secret), January 24, 1989, in AGF, F. 3, Dok. 7179, Ll. 1–3.

[115] Ibid., Ll. 2–3 (emphasis in original).

policy and national security, asking them to work together in compiling a critical appraisal of "the USSR's current obligations to provide military assistance to foreign countries, including under extreme circumstances."[116] Top experts from the Soviet Foreign Ministry and Defense Ministry, with input from a few other ministries and party and government agencies, jointly produced a detailed study of major aspects of the issue that in effect repudiated the Soviet government's earlier interpretations of its multilateral obligations under the Warsaw Treaty and its bilateral obligations to each of the East European countries.

On March 25, 1989, Gorbachev received a ten-page memorandum from Foreign Minister Shevardnadze, Defense Minister Yazov, and State Foreign Economic Commission Chairman Vladimir Kamentsev summarizing the findings of the review and laying out a series of far-reaching recommendations for changes in Soviet policy.[117] According to the memorandum, "the extreme circumstances that might trigger the provision of military assistance [to a Warsaw Pact country] pertain only to foreign threats, that is, situations when the right to individual or collective self-defense is carried out in accordance with Article 51 of the UN Charter." The document said that even "in the case of an armed attack" from outside, the "relevant provisions" in the Warsaw Treaty regarding collective defense were "flexible and did not automatically require the provision of military assistance." The Soviet Union's bilateral treaties with East European countries were "more definite" in calling for "the immediate provision of all manner of assistance, including military aid," but this was true only when "needed to defend [an ally] against external armed attack."[118]

Shevardnadze, Yazov, and Kamentsev stressed that "internal situations in the [Warsaw Pact] countries ... do not fall into the category" of contingencies covered by the Warsaw Treaty or by the bilateral defense treaties linking the Soviet Union with individual Warsaw Pact states "and therefore do not require us to take any sorts of measures in connection with our treaty obligations." Of particular importance in this regard were two of the USSR's East European allies: Czechoslovakia, which had been subject to strict "normalization" after the Soviet-led invasion in

---

[116] "Zapiska," from V. Zagladin to E. Shevardnadze, D. Yazov, and V. Kamentsev, January 27, 1989, in AGF, F. 3, Dok. 7179a., L. 1, with attachment.

[117] "Tovarishchu Gorbachevu M. S.," Memorandum No. 242/OS (Top Secret) to M. S. Gorbachev from E. Shevardnadze, D. Yazov, and V. Kamentsev, March 25, 1989, in Hoover Institution Archives (Stanford University), Papers of Vitalii Leonidovich Kataev, Box 13, Folder 14, pp. 1–10. Vitalii Kataev was deputy head of the CPSU Defense Industry Department (renamed Defense Department in 1991) during the Gorbachev era and served as an adviser to the CPSU General Secretary on military issues, arms control, and weapons production. Before he died in 2001, he and his daughter had arranged for copies of his papers to be transferred to the Hoover Institution, which acquired them in 2002. Five of the twenty boxes of papers have not yet been released, but all the rest are accessible.

[118] Ibid., pp. 1–2.

August 1968, and the German Democratic Republic (GDR), the Communist-ruled state in the East. The memorandum noted that "two of the [Soviet Union's bilateral] treaties – those with Czechoslovakia and the GDR – contain clauses about the defense of people's socialist gains," and the three Soviet officials acknowledged that these clauses "are construed in the West as codifying a right to the collective defense of socialism, including the use of military force, against internal as well as external threats." This was indeed the way Western observers had always interpreted those clauses in the two treaties, and it was also the way Soviet leaders had construed them prior to 1989. Shevardnadze, Yazov, and Kamentsev argued that such interpretations were invalid and that "the language in [the USSR's treaties with Czechoslovakia and the GDR] is in fact very general and does not automatically require military assistance to be provided."[119]

The three officials argued that "the phrasing of the Warsaw Treaty concerning the provision of military assistance is adequate for the current situation in the world and does not necessitate the adoption of any sorts of changes." They added that

> although the obligations contained in the USSR's bilateral treaties with allied states are formulated more strictly and could be construed in ways undesirable for us, it would not be appropriate for us to take the initiative in suggesting modifications or a reexamination of the treaties, in light of the travails being experienced by these states and the complex processes under way in them. Such an initiative might result in a weakening of allied relations and exacerbate the centrifugal trends in the [socialist] community and facilitate the destabilization of the situation in several of the countries.[120]

The memorandum went on to say that "if the question of reexamining a bilateral treaty is raised by the allied state itself, as is now being done by Bulgaria, then of course we should pursue the task of clarifying the treaty's terms, albeit without detriment to the allied obligations laid out therein." The three officials said that "concretely what we have in mind is to include in any new bilateral treaties [with Warsaw Pact countries in Eastern Europe] the phrasing that now appears in the Warsaw Treaty regarding the provision of [Soviet] military assistance" to a country under external attack.[121]

Zagladin's original memorandum to Gorbachev on January 24 had proposed that "after carrying out a review [of the USSR's military obligations] and taking account of the results of this review, we could consider raising this matter in strict confidence with the American side."[122] Gorbachev did not reject the idea, and Zagladin subsequently recommended to Shevardnadze, Yazov, and Kamentsev that the Soviet Union "should discuss with the American side on a confidential

---

[119] Ibid. [120] Ibid., p. 5. [121] Ibid., p. 6.
[122] "Dokladnaya zapiska o peresmotre obyazatel'stv po okazaniyu voennoi pomoshchi," Ll. 3.

basis [the USSR's] obligations concerning the provision of military assistance to allies."[123] The implication was that they should privately let U.S. officials know that the Soviet Union would no longer be coming to the aid of East European regimes faced with severe internal crises.

Shevardnadze, Yazov, and Kamentsev said they found Zagladin's proposal to be of "dubious merit," not only because "the USA would promptly inform its [NATO] allies about such discussions" but also because any confidential discussions about the matter "inevitably would be leaked to the press and we would appear in the eyes of our [Warsaw Pact] allies to be conspiring behind their backs with the United States regarding our obligations to our allies. The political effect of this [in Eastern Europe] would be extremely negative." Although Shevardnadze, Yazov, and Kamentsev expressed strong support for "the further positive development of the Soviet-American dialogue," they warned against explicitly taking up such sensitive matters with the U.S. government and argued that Soviet officials should instead pursue discussions in a more general way with their U.S. counterparts regarding how the two sides could "constructively facilitate the regulation of concrete problems that currently exist or could soon arise in various regions of the world."[124]

Even though Zagladin's proposal was not ultimately adopted, the mere fact that he had broached the idea underscores the firmness of the Soviet Union's decision in 1989 to avoid the use of military force in Eastern Europe and illustrates how much the international context of Soviet–East European relations had changed during the Gorbachev era. In the past, especially during the halcyon days of U.S. "rollback" and "liberation" rhetoric in the 1950s, the zero-sum nature of the Cold War rivalry would have caused Soviet leaders to fear that even the slightest relaxation of Soviet control in Eastern Europe would be exploited by the United States and other NATO countries at Moscow's expense.[125] No Soviet official prior to the late 1980s would ever have suggested holding confidential discussions with the U.S. government about possible Soviet responses to political crises in Eastern Europe. Since 1985, however, the rapid improvement of East–West relations had given Soviet leaders ample confidence that the United States and its NATO allies were no longer trying to undermine vital Soviet political-military interests in Eastern Europe.

Indeed, this very matter had come up explicitly in bilateral talks in mid-January 1989 (shortly before Zagladin sent his memorandum to Gorbachev) when former U.S. Secretary of State Henry Kissinger traveled to Moscow unofficially on

---

[123] "Zapiska" (see note 116 *supra*).
[124] "Tovarishchu Gorbachevu M. S." (see note 117 *supra*), p. 9.
[125] See, for example, Khrushchev's comments in late October 1956 about the U.S. government's malevolent designs vis-à-vis Hungary, cited in Kramer, "The Soviet Union and the 1956 Crises in Hungary and Poland," p. 191.

behalf of the Trilateral Commission with the knowledge and quiet blessing of the incoming U.S. administration of George H. W. Bush.[126] Kissinger's confidential discussions with Gorbachev and Yakovlev focused on, among other things, Soviet policy toward Eastern Europe in the context of U.S.–Soviet relations. In a conversation with Yakovlev, Kissinger proposed that senior U.S. and Soviet officials begin a secret "political dialogue" that would help to promote "political evolution" in Eastern Europe in an orderly way, eliminating the "potential for instability." The aim would be to alleviate the "dangerously volatile conditions" in the region and to avert any "political explosions" that would be damaging to everyone. According to Yakovlev's memorandum summarizing the conversation, Kissinger reported that he had "discussed this matter in detail with G. Bush's entourage," and that "the incoming U.S. administration would be ready to discuss these questions in a confidential format" while "taking full account of [the USSR's] legitimate security interests" in Eastern Europe.[127] Gorbachev promptly surmised, as he later told the CPSU Politburo, that Kissinger was in effect advocating "a U.S.-Soviet condominium in Europe" with "Finlandization" as a model for Eastern Europe – a largely accurate characterization of Kissinger's intent (though not necessarily of any specific measures the incoming Bush administration would have been willing to embrace in public).[128]

Although Gorbachev clearly welcomed Kissinger's proposal, he expressed concern that it would give the impression of "an attempt at collusion between the USSR and the USA at the expense of Europe." When Shevardnadze, Yazov, and Kamentsev recommended against Zagladin's proposal, the reasons they cited were not that the United States was hellbent on fomenting or taking advantage of the turmoil in Eastern Europe. Instead, the problem, as they (and Gorbachev) saw it, was the opposite – namely, that relations between the United States and USSR had warmed so much over the past few years that East European leaders would be inclined to suspect that U.S. and Soviet officials were conniving behind the backs of the East European governments to promote the superpowers' common interest in the region's fate. The far-reaching improvement of U.S.–Soviet relations was thus conducive to innovative Soviet actions vis-à-vis Eastern Europe – actions that would have been inconceivable at any previous stage of the Cold War.

---

[126] On the Kissinger-Gorbachev talks, see Jack F. Matlock, Jr., *Autopsy on an Empire: The American Ambassador's Account of the Collapse of the Soviet Union* (New York: Random House, 1995), pp. 190–192.

[127] "Zapis' besedy A. N. Yakovleva s G. Kissindzherom (SShA) 16 yanvarya 1989 g. po mezhdunarodnym problemam," Summary Transcript of conversation (Secret), January 17, 1989, in Gosudarstvennyi Arkhiv Rossiiskoi Federatsii (GARF), F. 10063, Op. 1, D. 258, Ll. 1–5.

[128] "Zapis' zasedaniya Politbyuro TsK KPSS, 24 yanvarya 1989 goda," Transcript of CPSU Politburo Session (Top Secret), January 24, 1989, in AGF, F. 10, Op. 2, Ll. 198–199.

The Dissolution of East European Communism

The increasing boldness of Gorbachev's pronouncements about Eastern Europe, combined with the publication of harsh reappraisals of earlier Soviet policies in the region (including the Brezhnev Doctrine), fueled the ongoing political spillover from the USSR into the other Soviet-bloc countries. As the pace of *perestroika* and *glasnost* accelerated in the Soviet Union, the "winds of change" gradually filtered throughout the Eastern bloc, bringing long-submerged grievances and social discontent to the surface. Under mounting popular pressure, the authorities in Hungary and Poland embarked on a wide range of ambitious reforms in 1988–1989 – more ambitious than what Gorbachev himself was pursuing. Rather than seeking to discourage or roll back the radical changes in Poland and Hungary, Gorbachev did just the opposite by praising developments in the two countries. In contrast to Gorbachev's first few years in office, when his public statements amounted to little more than standard pledges not to interfere in the domestic affairs of the East European states, by mid-1989 he was moving far beyond that and was no longer watering down anything he said. In a speech before the Council of Europe in July 1989, he expressed support for the maintenance of socialism in Europe, but then indicated a willingness to accept whatever result might come:

> The social and political orders of certain countries [in Europe] changed in the past, and may change again in the future. However, this is exclusively a matter for the peoples themselves to decide; it is their choice. Any interference in internal affairs, or any attempts to limit the sovereignty of states – including friends and allies, or anyone else – are impermissible.[129]

Against the backdrop of the remarkable changes under way in Poland and Hungary, including the imminent formation of a Polish government led by Solidarity (the independent mass movement that was banned in Poland from December 1981 until early 1989), this declaration took on even greater importance. Although the four other Warsaw Pact countries – Czechoslovakia, East Germany, Romania, and to a lesser extent Bulgaria – staunchly eschewed any hint of liberalization and clung firmly to orthodox Communist policies, there was no doubt by early to mid-1989 that Gorbachev was willing to permit far-reaching internal political changes in Eastern Europe that previously would have been ruled out and forcibly suppressed under the Brezhnev Doctrine.

The radical implications of Gorbachev's approach were evident when the drastic reforms adopted in Hungary and Poland proceeded without letup,

---

[129] "Rech' M. S. Gorbacheva," *Izvestiya* (Moscow), July 7, 1989, p. 2. For an English translation of the speech, see "Address Given by Mikhail Gorbachev to the Council of Europe (July 6, 1989)," in Council of Europe, Parliamentary Assembly, *Official Report*, 41st Ordinary Sess., May-July 1989, Vol. 1, pp. 197–205.

culminating in the formation of a Solidarity-led government in Poland in August 1989 and the advent of a multiparty system in Hungary. But the full magnitude of the forces unleashed by Gorbachev's policies did not become apparent until the final few months of 1989. Events that would have been unthinkable even a year or two earlier suddenly happened – peaceful revolutions from below in East Germany and Czechoslovakia, the dismantling of the Berlin Wall, popular ferment and the downfall of Todor Zhivkov in Bulgaria, and violent upheaval and the execution of Nicolae and Elena Ceauşescu in Romania.

As one orthodox Communist regime after another collapsed, the Soviet Union reacted calmly and expressed support for the reformist, non-Communist governments that emerged in the Warsaw Pact countries. Soviet leaders also joined their East European counterparts in condemning previous instances of Soviet interference in Eastern Europe, particularly the invasion of Czechoslovakia in August 1968.[130] Before Gorbachev came to power, the USSR had done all it could to stifle and deter political liberalization in Eastern Europe; but by late 1989 there was no doubt that the East European countries had full leeway to pursue fundamental political, economic, and social reforms, including the option of abandoning Communism and embracing Western-style democracy.

For the Warsaw Pact, the sweeping reorientation of Soviet policy in Eastern Europe proved to have devastating consequences. After dozens of Soviet marshals and generals were ousted in early 1989, the officers who replaced them were responsible for trying to adapt the alliance to the dramatic changes sweeping through Eastern Europe and the USSR. Earlier measures connected with the implementation of the Pact's defensive doctrine were beginning to erode the Warsaw Pact's military capabilities, but the fate of the alliance was ultimately determined by political, not military, considerations. Meetings of the PCC, the Warsaw Pact Committee of Foreign Ministers, and the Warsaw Pact Committee of Defense Ministers in 1989 were inevitably buffeted by the rush of developments in both Eastern Europe and the Soviet Union. When the PCC convened in July 1989, the formal proceedings had a surreal quality. The assembled leaders stuck largely to formulaic discussions and issued a communiqué consisting entirely of boilerplate language. Only during breaks and on the sidelines of the meeting did the participants discuss the sweeping changes under way in Poland and Hungary and the potential transformation of the entire Soviet bloc.[131]

---

[130] "Zayavlenie rukovoditelei Bolgarii, Vengrii, GDR, Pol'shi, i Sovetskogo Soyuza" and "Zayavlenie Sovetskogo pravitel'stva," *Izvestiya* (Moscow), December 5, 1989, p. 2.

[131] See the stark first-hand account by Heinz Keßler, the East German defense minister in 1989, in *Zur Sache und zur Person*, pp. 244–247. A first-rate collection of translated materials on this meeting are available in Mastny and Byrne, eds., *A Cardboard Castle?* pp. 644–654.

The Fate of the Soviet Bloc's Military Alliance

It is no small irony that as Communism was disintegrating in Eastern Europe, the only Warsaw Pact leader who explicitly called on the alliance to take military action to roll back the tide was Nicolae Ceaușescu of Romania, who claimed that the emergence of a Solidarity-led government in Poland would benefit "imperialist, reactionary forces" and "jeopardize the interests of socialism, including the Warsaw Pact."[132] In a striking reversal of his position in 1968 when he opposed the Soviet-led invasion of Czechoslovakia, Ceaușescu in August 1989 secretly urged the other Warsaw Pact states to join Romania in sending troops to Poland to prevent Solidarity from coming to power:

> As a Communist party and socialist country, [we] cannot consider this to be solely a Polish internal affair. [We] believe it concerns all socialist countries.... The Communist and workers' parties of the socialist countries, representing the members of the Warsaw Pact, should adopt a stance and demand that Solidarity not be entrusted with the mission of forming a government. [We] have decided to appeal to ... the leaders of the parties in the Warsaw Pact countries and other socialist countries to express serious concern and to ask for joint [military] action to avert the grave situation in Poland and to defend socialism and the Polish people.[133]

Soviet leaders immediately dismissed any such notion and lodged a stern protest with Ceaușescu, whose relationship with Gorbachev had long been uneasy and strained.[134] Ceaușescu had sought to gain the PZPR's backing for joint Warsaw Pact action against Solidarity, but Polish Communist leaders had promptly rejected and condemned the "invitation." Soviet officials thereupon told the Romanians that "the PZPR is better qualified than anyone to judge whether such action would be worthwhile," and that Ceaușescu should "heed the PZPR's advice" and drop the matter.[135] The Soviet Politburo warned the Romanians that the USSR would refuse

---

[132] "De la Varşovia," *Scînteia* (Bucharest), August 20, 1989, p. 1.

[133] The full text of Romania's appeal, dated August 19, 1989 (the same day that Mazowiecki was officially invited to form a government in Warsaw), is reproduced in "Dokumenty: Polska-Rumunia," *Gazeta Wyborcza* (Warsaw), September 29 – October 1, 1989, p. 6. This bizarre episode was reported at length in the same issue of *Gazeta Wyborcza*.

[134] "Postanovlenie Politbyuro Tsentral'nogo Komiteta KPSS No. P164/132: Ob obrashchenii t. N. Chaushesku," CPSU Politburo Resolution No. 164/132 (Top Secret), August 21, 1989, in RGANI, F. 5, Op. 102, D. 180, Ll. 2, 6–7, 63; "Postanovlenie Politbyuro Tsentral'nogo Komiteta KPSS No. P164/169: Ob otvete rumynskomu rukovodstvu na predlozhenie o provedenii vstrechi rukovoditelei bratskikh partii sotsialisticheskikh po voprosu o polozhenii v Pol'she," CPSU Politburo Resolution No. P164/169 (Top Secret), August 21, 1989, in RGANI, F. 5, Op. 102, D. 180, Ll. 2, 7, 76; and "Otvet rumynskomu rukovodstvu na predlozhenie o provedenii vstrechi dlya obsuzhdeniya o polozhenii v Pol'she," Draft Letter (Top Secret) from CPSU Politburo to Nicolae Ceaușescu, August 21, 1989, in RGANI, F. 5, Op. 102, D. 181, Ll. 140–141.

[135] "Otvet rumynskomu rukovodstvu na predlozhenie," L. 140. In Hungary the authorities expressed even sharper criticism of the Romanian proposal. See "Jegyzőkönyv az Elnökség 1989. augusztus 21-én megtartott üléséről: 7. A Román Kommunista Párt és Nicolae Ceaușescu

to "take any steps that would vitiate Poland's sovereignty," a position that Ceaușescu himself had long championed until August 1989.

From then on, as the East European populations increasingly sensed that their actions would not provoke Soviet/Warsaw Pact military intervention, they took to the streets to demand an end to Communist rule. Hardline leaders in Eastern Europe had assumed that, in extremis, the Soviet Union would intervene to maintain Communist regimes in the region, and they were shocked when they finally realized this would not be the case. Their own will to stay in power – by any means necessary – evaporated as they came to understand they were facing a hopeless situation. What followed was the swift and largely peaceful collapse of Communism in Eastern Europe.

Disbandment of the Warsaw Pact

Even before the Warsaw Pact was formally abolished on the 1st of July 1991, the lingering effectiveness of the alliance had disappeared. The fundamental political changes that occurred in Eastern Europe in 1989 and 1990 – changes that the Warsaw Pact in earlier decades was supposed to prevent, especially in the GDR – deprived the alliance of its main raison d'être. Soviet officials themselves privately acknowledged in early 1990 that the upheavals in Eastern Europe had "shifted the military balance on the European continent in favor of the West."[136] Some in Moscow concluded at an early stage that the shift in the military balance was "fundamental" and "decisive," especially with the prospect that a unified Germany would be integrated into NATO. Others at first were hopeful that the Soviet Union could "limit [its] 'losses'" by "promoting the formation of an all-European security system" that would supplant both NATO and the Warsaw Pact.[137] It soon became clear, however, that no such system was actually going to materialize.

Initially, some East European officials and national security experts, especially in Hungary and Czechoslovakia, were allured by the prospect of a pan-European security organization that would replace both the Warsaw Pact and NATO. But as they examined the issue more closely in the first half of 1990, they concluded that a fundamental disparity had emerged between the two alliances, making it impossible to replace the two together, especially in the absence of a security organization that would have truly pan-European

---

üzenete a magyar vezetéshez a lengyelorszagli eseményekkel kapcsolatban," MSZMP Elnökség 1989/141 (Top Secret), August 21, 1989, in Hoover Institution Archives (Stanford University), Imre Pozsgay Papers, Box 45, Folder MSZMP Elnöksége, 1989, Group 5.

[136] "Voenno-politicheskie aspekty obstanovki v Evrope (Analiticheskaya zapiska)," prepared by the Soviet Foreign Ministry's Directorate on Arms Control and Disarmament, n.d. (c. early March 1990), in AGF, F. 2, Op. 2, Dok. 1012, Ll. 1–16.

[137] Ibid., Ll. 1, 2.

military forces.[138] As a result, the East European governments increasingly sought to loosen their ties (political as well as military) with the Warsaw Pact and to move toward NATO, including with the goal of eventual membership in the alliance.

Under these circumstances, Soviet and East European leaders' views about the future of the Warsaw Pact steadily diverged in the latter half of 1990. Until 1991, Soviet officials were still hoping they could preserve the Pact's political councils, whereas policymakers in Hungary and Czechoslovakia (and eventually in Poland as well) increasingly felt that the entire alliance had to be dismantled, not just the military forces.[139] In the latter half of 1990, they tried to expedite the process, though with limited success. But events in the USSR in December 1990 and especially January 1991 – the abrupt resignation of Foreign Minister Shevardnadze as he spoke with alarm about a coming hardline backlash in Moscow, a forceful speech by KGB Chairman Vladimir Kryuchkov warning that "blood might have to be spilled" to restore order in the country, and a forceful crackdown in Lithuania and Latvia by the Soviet Army and KGB – brought matters to a head, inducing the East European governments to push for an end to the Warsaw Pact as soon as possible.

On January 21, 1991, barely 24 hours after the violent Soviet crackdown in Latvia, the foreign ministers of Czechoslovakia, Hungary, and Poland met in Budapest to discuss security arrangements and how to contend with the resurgence of hardliners in Moscow. They issued a joint statement affirming that their countries would pull out of the Warsaw Pact unless the Soviet Union agreed to convene a long-delayed PCC meeting to plan for the dismantling of the alliance's military structures.[140] Faced with this prospect, Gorbachev reluctantly agreed that the PCC conclave should be held in Budapest on February 25, 1991 at the level of foreign and defense ministers.[141]

Soviet military officers tried to sway the outcome of the PCC meeting by warning in advance of "dire consequences" if the Warsaw Pact were dissolved "prematurely" as a "political-military alliance." The first deputy chief of the Soviet General Staff, Army-General Vladimir Lobov, asserted that the elimination of the

---

[138] Mark Kramer, "NATO, Russia, and East European Security," in Uri Ra'anan and Kate Martin, eds., *Russia: A Return to Imperialism?* (New York: St. Martin's Press, 1995), pp. 105–160.

[139] Békés, "Hungary and the Dissolution of the Warsaw Pact," pp. 4–23.

[140] Kazimierz Woycicki, "Szansa dla Europy Środkowej: Zbliżenie polsko-czechosłowacko-węgierskie," *Życie Warszawy* (Warsaw), January 22, 1991, pp. 1, 4. This move had been prefigured a week before the meeting in an interview with György Keleti of the Hungarian Defense Ministry, in "A Varsói Szerződeést tárgyalásos úton kívánjuk ielszámolni: Keleti György a honvédség feladatairól," *Magyar Nemzet* (Budapest), January 15, 1991, p. 4.

[141] It took nearly another three weeks, until February 11, before Gorbachev formally proposed the Budapest meeting See "Pametna zapiska ot Neicho Neichev, zam. Nachalnik na otdel 'OMV'," Memorandum No. 93-N-17 (Secret), February 11, 1991, from Neicho Neichev, in Arhiv na Ministerstvoto na vutreshnite raboti (AMVR), Sofia, Op. 48–10, D. 38, L. 4.

Pact's military command and the withdrawal of Soviet troops from Eastern Europe would make it "all but impossible [for the Soviet Army] to fulfill the requirements of the concept of 'defense sufficiency'" and would remove "the only force in Europe that can offset the military potential of NATO."[142] In an interview published two days before the Budapest gathering, the commander-in-chief of the Pact, Army-General Petr Lushev, argued that the Soviet Union and its allies must remain fully ready to counter NATO:

> [The NATO governments] are speaking a good deal about the need to preserve a "counterbalance to the USSR's military potential" and about the risk of an impending civil war in the [Soviet] Union. This is the general state of things. Under these pretexts, NATO is busy taking measures to upgrade its military structures. Moreover, it is hardly a secret that the United States has always viewed Russia and the USSR as its geopolitical rival. We must keep this in mind when we discuss our country's defense capabilities.... Unfortunately, the task of relying solely on political means to preserve peace nowadays is not always possible.[143]

Lushev's comments were echoed by Soviet Defense Minister Yazov, who insisted that the elimination of the Pact would "fundamentally alter the strategic-military situation on the continent" and would undercut "Soviet security interests."[144] Although Yazov by this time realized there was no longer any chance of preserving the military component of the alliance, he evidently hoped that the political structures could be maintained and even expanded for at least another year or two.

These last-ditch attempts to prevent the outright dissolution of the Warsaw Pact proved futile. The demise of the Pact, far from being deferred, was accelerated by the Budapest meeting on February 25. The meeting, attended by the foreign and defense ministers of the six countries, lasted only three hours. After a series of brief prepared statements, the participants signed a document stipulating that all allied military institutions would be disbanded by the end of March.[145] They also confirmed that a final meeting of the PCC would be held in

---

[142] Army-General V. I Lobov, "Puti realizatsii kontseptsii dostatochnosti dlya oborony," *Voennaya mysl'* (Moscow), No. 2, February 1991, p.16.

[143] Interview with Lushev in "U nas svoya chest'," *Sovetskaya Rossiya* (Moscow), February 23, 1991, pp. 1–2.

[144] Interview with Yazov in "Sluzhu Sovetskomu Soyuzu!" *Pravda* (Moscow), February 23, 1991, pp. 1–2. See also Yazov's article "Pobeda: Pamyat' i pobeda," *Pravda* (Moscow), May 9, 1991, p. 3. For a more optimistic view by a younger officer, see Major M. Zheglov, "Varshavskii Dogovor i evropeiskaya bezopasnost'," *Krasnaya zvezda* (Moscow), February 22, 1991, p. 3. Although Zheglov conceded that the end of Soviet–East European military ties would pose "substantial problems for [Soviet] security," he argued that "it makes no sense to preserve a military alliance if the states belonging to it do not voluntarily desire to maintain their relations."

[145] "Protokol o prekrashchenii deistviya voennykh soglashenii, zaklyuchennykh v ramkakh Varshavskogo Dogovora, i uprazdnenii ego voennykh organov i struktur," text and signatures reproduced in A. I. Gribkov, *Sud'ba Varshavskogo Dogovora: Vospominaniya, dokumenty,*

Prague by mid-1991 to abolish the remaining political structures of the alliance (subsequently, the date of the meeting was set for July 1). Any lingering hopes in Moscow that the East European states would be willing to keep the PCC as a political forum for a lengthy "transitional" period were thereby dashed.[146]

Although this outcome had been largely expected, it triggered vehement complaints in Moscow among hardline Soviet Communist Party officials and military commanders, who condemned "our Warsaw Pact allies for refusing to cooperate with us on matters of fundamental importance."[147] To help offset the loss of the Pact's military structures, the Soviet High Command launched a reassessment of its military doctrine and encouraged the Soviet parliament to defer the passage of legislation regarding force reductions and other military reforms that had been championed by Gorbachev.[148] In addition, the Soviet Defense Ministry stepped up its efforts to "prevent our former military allies from joining other military alliances and groupings, above all NATO, and from taking part in any arrangements that would lead to the deployment of foreign troops on their territory."[149]

Soviet officials followed up on these sentiments in the spring of 1991 by seeking to conclude new bilateral treaties with the East European countries to replace the interlocking agreements between the Soviet Union and the other

---

fakty (Moscow: Russkaya kniga, 1998), pp. 198–200. Point 3 of this four-point protocol stipulates that Warsaw Pact "documents are not to be transmitted to third parties or disseminated." This provision later became controversial because it was cited by Russian archivists and by the Russian Ministry of Defense as a justification for denying access to the records of the Warsaw Pact. The provision also was cited by the Polish government to explain its refusal to declassify large numbers of military documents from the Communist era. Not until 2006 did the Polish government change its position on the matter, opening access for researchers to all Warsaw Pact records. Unlike tin Russia and Poland, the Hungarian, Czechoslovak (and later Czech and Slovak), and Bulgarian governments began soon after 1991 to grant expansive access to their Communist-era military records, including items pertaining to the Warsaw Pact. The same was true in Germany, where East German records pertaining to the Warsaw Pact were promptly made available.

[146] "A VSZ valamennyi katonai szervezete megszűnik: Véget ért a tankkötelezettség," *Népszava* (Budapest), February 26, 1991, pp. 1, 3; and "Lépés egy összeurópai biztonsági rendszer felé," *Népszabadság* (Budapest), February 26, 1991, p. 6.

[147] "Na nachalakh razumnoi i nadezhnoi dostatochnosti dlya oborony," *Krasnaya zvezda* (Moscow), April 4, 1991, p. 2. See also Colonel V. Markushin, "Ot lyubvi do nenavisti? Chto trevozhit v pozitsii nekotorykh vostochnoevropeiskikh sosedei," *Krasnaya zvezda* (Moscow), February 5, 1991, p. 3.

[148] Interview with Leonid Sharin, chairman of the Supreme Soviet Committee on Defense and Security, in "Dlya armii etot god budet perelomnym," *Krasnaya zvezda* (Moscow), April 17, 1991, p. 2.

[149] This phrasing comes from "O razvitii obstanovki v Vostochnoi Evrope i nashei politike v etom regione: Postanovlenie Sekretariata TsK Kommunisticheskoi Partii Sovetskogo Soyuza," No. St-15/2 (Secret), January 22, 1991, in RGANI, F. 89, Op. 45, D. 63, Ll. 1–9. The CPSU Secretariat resolution and the memorandum were subsequently declassified and published in *Izvestiya TsK KPSS* (Moscow), No. 3 (March 1991), pp. 12–17.

member-states of the Warsaw Pact. Although Soviet leaders claimed that the new treaties would be based on "equal rights, good neighborliness, and complete respect of mutual interests," they pressed for the inclusion of language that would commit each side "not to participate in a military-political alliance directed against the other side, and not to permit a third country to use the transport and communications systems or the infrastructure of one side against the other."[150] Soviet Foreign Ministry officials publicly admitted that these draft provisions were intended to prevent the East European countries from joining NATO.[151]

The Hungarian, Czechoslovak, Polish, and Bulgarian governments immediately rejected the proposed language as an "infringement of [their] sovereignty" and an "unacceptable attempt to restrict" their countries' "freedom to choose whether to join security alliances."[152] The leaders of Hungary, Poland, Czechoslovakia, and Bulgaria stressed that the "gradual integration" of their countries into NATO was "inevitable" and that "any bilateral treaty we sign with the Soviet Union must not hinder us in negotiating and consulting with [the Western alliance] and eventually joining it."[153] They warned that if the offending clauses were not omitted from the draft bilateral treaties, they would refuse to sign: "It would be better to have no treaty at all than to accept a bad one."[154]

Although the Romanian government did prove willing in April 1991 to sign a bilateral treaty that obligated each side not to join a "hostile military alliance"

---

[150] The first quoted passage is from "Ne nado dramatizirovat'," *Izvestiya* (Moscow), May 7, 1991, p. 3. The second quoted passage is from Fedor Luk'yanov, "My ne khotim byt' neitral'nymi, zayavil vengerskii prem'er," *Izvestiya* (Moscow), May 1, 1991, p. 4.

[151] Interview with Soviet Deputy Foreign Minister Yulii Kvitsinskii in "Magyar-szovjet tárgyalások: Időrekord helyett jó szerződést," *Népszabadság* (Budapest), April 29, 1991, pp. 1, 3. See also the interview with Sergei Karaganov, then deputy director of the USSR's European Studies Institute, in "Az utolsó katonavonat Eperjeskén," *Magyar Hirlap* (Budapest), June 15, 1991, p. 8. For a strong critique of this Soviet policy by a prominent "new thinker" affiliated with Aleksandr Yakovlev, see Mikhail Kozhokin, "Kreml' ozhidaet mnogogo ot byvshikh soyuznikov," *Moskovskie novosti* (Moscow), No. 22 (June 2, 1991), p. 3.

[152] Luk'yanov, "My ne khotim byt' neitral'nymi," p. 4; "Zayavlenie prezidenta ChSFR," *Izvestiya* (Moscow), April 30, 1991, p. 1; "Podpishet li Bolgariya dogovor?" *Izvestiya* (Moscow), May 1, 1991, p. 1; "Nyama predvaritelni usloviya za razgovorite mezhdu Popov i Pavlov," *Otechestven vestnik* (Sofia), May 16, 1991, pp. 1–2; interview with Polish Foreign Minister Krzysztof Skubiszewski in "Két hatalom közé ékelődve: Interjú a lengyel külügyminiszterrel," *Népszabadság* (Budapest), June 6, 1991, pp. 1, 6; and interview with Hungarian Deputy Defense Minister György Keleti in "Keleti ezredes a katonai szerződésről," *Népszabadság* (Budapest), June 14, 1991, p. 5. See also Alfred Reisch, "Hungary: The Hard Task of Setting Relations with the USSR on a New Footing," *Radio Free Europe Report on Eastern Europe*, Vol. 2, No. 20 (May 24, 1991), esp. pp. 15–19; and Suzanne Crow, "Negotiating New Treaties with Eastern Europe," *Radio Liberty Report on the USSR*, Vol. 2, No. 28 (July 19, 1991), pp. 3–6.

[153] Interview with István Körmendi, head of the European department of the Hungarian Foreign Ministry, in "NATO: A Szovjetunió beléphet," *Magyar Hirlap* (Budapest), February 28, 1991, p. 3.

[154] Interview with Hungarian Foreign Minister Géza Jeszenszky in "Ugrás a sötétbe: Vállalatvezetűk a szovjet kapcsolatról," *Beszélő* (Budapest), May 25, 1991, p. 9.

in the future, Romanian leaders claimed that this phrasing was directed only against "offensive" alliances and not against a "defensive" alliance like NATO.[155] They insisted that "Romania retains complete freedom to participate in alliances of a defensive nature," including NATO.[156] Soviet officials brushed aside these disavowals and warmly praised the new agreement with Romania, calling it a "model for good-neighborly security relations." However, the Soviet–Romanian treaty was the only one that ultimately proved feasible. All the other East European governments staunchly resisted Soviet pressure.

On July 1, 1991, Soviet and East European leaders gathered in Prague for the final meeting of the PCC. For symbolic reasons, Gorbachev declined to attend the meeting and sent his vice president, Gennadii Yanaev, in his place. Czechoslovak President Václav Havel chaired the session, which began with prepared statements by Yanaev and the other participants, who sought to move matters along expeditiously.[157] The six leaders then signed a document liquidating the Warsaw Pact. The document stressed that the Pact was being eliminated because of "the profound changes in Europe that have brought an end to confrontation and to the division of the continent."[158] By all accounts, the East European leaders were "elated" when the PCC meeting adjourned.

In Moscow, however, reactions to the disbandment of the alliance were far more mixed. On the one hand, officials from the Soviet Foreign Ministry sought to put the outcome in the best possible light. Foreign Minister Aleksandr Bessmertnykh argued that the dissolution of the Pact would help rather than impair Soviet security:

> Defense outlays for the Soviet Union will now be lower because we will be required to defend only our own borders and security interests. Up to now it has cost us a substantial amount of money to underwrite the Warsaw Pact.... Henceforth, we can focus our resources on the strengthening of our own defense and security.[159]

---

[155] For the text of the 23-article treaty, including the relevant clause, see "Tratat de colaborare, bună vecinătate, și amiciție între România Uniunea Republicilor Sovietice Socialiste," *România Liberă* (Bucharest), April 12, 1991, p. 8. See also Vladimir Socor, "The Romanian-Soviet Friendship Treaty and Its Regional Implications," *Radio Free Europe Report on Eastern Europe*, Vol. 2, No. 17 (May 3, 1991), pp. 25–33.

[156] B. Rodionov, "Nakhodit' vzaimopriemlemye formuly: Kakimi budut dogovory SSSR s sosedyami v Vostochnoi Evrope," *Izvestiya* (Moscow), June 4, 1991, p. 5.

[157] For a first-hand chronicle of the meeting by one of Havel's aides who took part, see Zdeněk Matějka, "How the Warsaw Pact Was Dissolved," *Perspectives*, No. 8 (Summer 1997), pp. 55–65.

[158] "Protokol o prekrashchenii deistviya Dogovora o druzhbe, sotrudnichestve i vzaimnoi pomoshchi, podpisannogo v Varshave 14 maya 1955 goda, i Protokola o prodlenii sroka ego deistviya, podpisannogo 26 aprelya 1985 goda v Varshave," *Izvestiya* (Moscow), July 3, 1991, p. 5.

[159] "Ministr inostrannykh del SSSR ob uprazdnenii Varshavskogo Dogovora i ego posledstviyakh dlya Evropy, SSSR, i polozhenii v Yugoslavii," *Izvestiya* (Moscow), July 4, 1991, p. 2.

The outlook among senior military officers was much more jaundiced. The Soviet Defense Ministry declined to send any of its personnel to the final meeting of the PCC, leaving it entirely to the Soviet presidential administration and the Foreign Ministry. When journalists contacted Yazov at his office in Moscow on July 1 shortly after the PCC meeting in Prague ended, he refused to answer any of their questions and insisted that "this event had absolutely nothing to do with the [Soviet] military."[160] A journalist who tried to follow up was asked to leave the ministry building.

The formal dissolution of the Warsaw Pact merely codified a process that had been under way since late 1990, when the alliance had ceased to function in any meaningful sense, leaving NATO as the only security organization in Europe. The elaborate command-and-control infrastructure that Soviet leaders had worked so long to develop for the Pact became defunct, and pressures quickly mounted for the withdrawal of all Soviet troops and weapons from the region.[161] In February 1990 the Soviet Union agreed to remove its entire Central and Southern Groups of Forces from Czechoslovakia and Hungary by July 1991, a schedule that many Soviet military officers believed was too compressed.[162] Marshal Kulikov later recalled the bitterness that he and other military commanders had felt about the pace of the withdrawals:

> To call it a give-away is putting it far too mildly. I would say it bordered on criminality. The decision to pull troops so quickly out of Hungary, Czechoslovakia, and especially Germany was rash and ill-conceived. The officer corps was left in a disastrous state, bereft of housing, material support, and the right to a new job. Everything was done in a slapdash manner.... I have to acknowledge that [we in] the military leadership were too docile; we were not perseverant enough and failed to insist that our troops should be pulled out in an orderly manner, with adequate support for our armed forces, the officer corps, and their families.[163]

---

[160] Cited on *Sobytiya dnya,* Russian Television Network, July 1, 1991; program tape stored at Cold War Studies Archive, Harvard University.

[161] S. F. Akhromeev and G. M. Kornienko, *Glazami marshala i diplomata* (Moscow: Mezhdunarodnye otnosheniya, 1992), p. 295.

[162] "Soglashenie mezhdu Pravitel'stvom Soyuza Sovetskikh Sotsialisticheskikh Respublik i Pravitel'stvom Chekhoslovatskoi Sotsialisticheskoi Respubliki o vyvode sovetskikh voisk s territorii Chekhoslovatskoi Sotsialisticheskoi Respubliki," *Vestnik Ministerstva inostrannykh del SSSR* (Moscow), No. 6 (March 31, 1990), pp. 4–5; and "Soglashenie mezhdu Pravitsl'stvom Soyuza Sovetskikh Sotsialisticheskikh Respublik i Pravitel'stvom Vengerskoi Respubliki o vyvode sovetskikh voisk, vremenno nakhodyashchikhsya na territorii Vengrii," March 9, 1990, supplement to "Postanovlenie TsK KPSS: O vyvode sovetskikh voisk iz Vengrii," K-227/OS (Secret), March 9, 1990, pp. 10–13, in RGANI, F. 89, Per. 8, D. 21, Ll. 1–8. The Hungarian and Czechoslovak governments initially had pressed for the withdrawals to be completed by the end of 1990. Only with reluctance did they settle for the mid-1991 deadline.

[163] Interview with Kulikov in Ekaterina Labetskaya, "Marshal Kulikov: 'Voennye byli slishkom poslushnymi'," *Vremya MN* (Moscow), September 6, 1999, p. 2.

Despite these sentiments (which some officers voiced in public), the withdrawals from Hungary and Czechoslovakia proceeded with great celerity over the next sixteen months, finishing slightly ahead of schedule. A provisional agreement regarding the Soviet Union's Northern Group of Forces was concluded with the Polish government in October 1991, and it was then reaffirmed in a formal Russian–Polish treaty in May 1992. Under that treaty, all combat soldiers from the ex-Soviet Army were taken out of Poland by the end of October 1992, and the small number of remaining logistical troops departed by September 1993.[164] The withdrawal of several hundred thousand Soviet/Russian troops and support personnel from eastern Germany was completed in September 1994, four months ahead of the timetable laid out in treaties signed a few weeks before German reunification in the fall of 1990.[165] The final pullout of forces from Germany eliminated the former Soviet Army's presence in Eastern Europe, thus completing the demise of the Warsaw Pact.

Conclusions

From the time the Warsaw Pact was founded in 1955, it was dominated by the Soviet Union. The East European members acquired a greater say in the Pact from the 1960s on and were able to influence Soviet leaders on numerous issues, but the Soviet Union had by far the greatest impact on the organization and routinely achieved what it wanted. To be sure, Soviet leaders did not always get their way even on crucial matters. Albania left the Warsaw Pact in the 1960s after engaging in a bitter dispute with the Soviet Union, and Romania began curtailing its role in the organization in the mid-1960s and periodically refused to go along with the other member-states on key issues such as the invasion of Czechoslovakia in August 1968 (which Ceaușescu publicly denounced) and the adoption in March 1980 of a unified command-and-control structure that would have given immense power in wartime to the Soviet marshals and generals who headed the alliance.[166]

The Soviet Union's preponderant role in the Warsaw Pact worked to Gorbachev's advantage after he became CPSU General Secretary in 1985. Upon taking office, he was hoping to strengthen the alliance under Soviet leadership, as his predecessors had done. But over time, as he increasingly sensed the enormous challenges he would have to overcome to revitalize the

---

[164] Marek Henzler and Włodzimierz Kalski, "Wyechali: Armia Radziecka z nami od dziecka," *Polityka* (Warsaw), No. 39 (September 25, 1993), pp. 12–13.
[165] "Dogovor ob okonchatel'nom uregulirovanii v otnoshenii Germanii,"*Izvestiya* (Moscow), September 13, 1990, p. 4.
[166] For translations of important declassified documents concerning Romania's refusal to go along with the Warsaw Pact's newly created command-and-control system for wartime, see CIA, *Warsaw Pact Wartime Statutes*.

Soviet economy, he shifted in favor of changes in Soviet policy toward Eastern Europe that had far-reaching implications for the Warsaw Pact. Initially, the steps he took were of minor importance, but by 1988 and especially early 1989 Gorbachev moved in a much more radical direction, adumbrating his larger effort to end the Cold War and foster an auspicious international climate for domestic economic reforms. The Soviet Union's dominant role in the Warsaw Pact enabled Gorbachev to avoid consulting with his East European counterparts before he renounced the Brezhnev Doctrine and abandoned the USSR's long-standing commitment to prop up orthodox Communist regimes in the Soviet bloc. When the CPSU Politburo secretly adopted its momentous resolution in late March 1989 ruling out the use of Soviet troops in Eastern Europe to defend Communist regimes against internal political unrest, Gorbachev and his colleagues decided not to inform East European leaders about the resolution, lest it demoralize them. Not until later that year, as domestic political upheavals began to sweep through Eastern Europe and precipitate the downfall of Communist rule, did hardliners in the Warsaw Pact finally realize that the Soviet Army would no longer be intervening on their behalf no matter how dire the circumstances they faced.

Events in 1989 moved so rapidly that Soviet officials initially did not appreciate how much the geopolitical situation in Eastern Europe had changed. Until the latter half of 1990, Gorbachev and other Soviet policy-makers were still hopeful and confident that the Warsaw Pact could be preserved as a political organization with some connection to security issues. Some officials in Eastern Europe, especially Poland, also initially thought the Warsaw Pact would survive, but by the summer of 1990, the East European governments increasingly believed they should push for the dissolution of the Pact as soon as possible. During the final year of the alliance's existence, the Soviet Union no longer enjoyed a dominant role in the organization. Leaders in Czechoslovakia, Hungary, and Poland took the initiative in late 1990 and early 1991, especially after the crackdown in the Soviet Baltic republics in January 1991. When the East European governments pressed for the disbandment of the alliance by mid-1991, Soviet officials had little choice but to go along. The Soviet Union continued to exist for another six months after the Warsaw Pact was dissolved, but the end of the alliance foreshadowed the collapse of the USSR itself.

Select Bibliography

Archival Repositories

Rossiiskii Gosudarstvennyi Arkhiv Noveishei Istorii (RGANI), Moscow.
Arkhiv Gorbachev-Fonda (AGF), Moscow.
Gosudarstvennyi Arkhiv Rossiiskoi Federatsii (GARF), Moscow.
Arkhiv Vneshnei Politiki Rossiiskoi Federatsii (AVPRF), Moscow.
Arkhiv Prezidenta Rossiiskoi Federatsii (APRF), Moscow.
Stiftung Archiv der Parteien und Massenorganisationen der DDR im Bundesarchiv (SAPMO-BA), Berlin.
Bundesarchiv – Abteilung Militärarchiv (BA – Abt. MA), Freiburg.
Národní Archiv České Republiky (NA ČR), Prague.
Archiv Bezpečnostních Složek (ABS), Prague.
Magyar Országos Levéltár (MOL), Budapest.
Archiwum Akt Nowych (AAN), Warsaw.
Centralne Archiwum Wojskowe (CAW), Warsaw.
Centralen Darzhaven Arhiv (CDA), Sofia.
Arhiv na Ministerstvoto na vutreshnite raboti (AMVR), Sofia.
Darzhaven Voennoistoricheski Arhiv (DVIA), Veliko Tarnovo.
Hoover Institution Archives (HIA), Stanford University, Stanford, CA.

Published Sources

"A Varsói Szerzűdeést tárgyalásos úton kívánjuk ielszámolni: Keleti György a honvédség feladatairól," *Magyar Nemzet* (Budapest), January 15, 1991, p. 4.
"A VSZ valamennyi katonai szervezete megszűnik: Véget ért a tankkötelezettség," *Népszava* (Budapest), February 26, 1991, pp. 1, 3.
"Ahonnan nem lehet elmenekülni, az ország peremén," *Heti Világgazdaság* (Budapest), No. 36 (August 16, 1986), pp. 7–8.
Akhromeev, S. F., and G. M. Kornienko. *Glazami marshala i diplomata* (Moscow: Mezhdunarodnye otnosheniya, 1992).
Albright, David, and Jiří Valenta, eds. *The Communist States in Africa* (Bloomington: Indiana University Press, 1982).
"Az utolsó katonavonat Eperjeskén," *Magyar Hirlap* (Budapest), June 15, 1991, p. 8.
Beissinger, Mark R. *Nationalist Mobilization and the Collapse of the Soviet State* (New York: Cambridge University Press, 2002).

Békés, Csaba. "Hungary and the Dissolution of the Warsaw Pact (1988–1991)," *Journal of Cold War Studies*, Vol. 25, No. 4 (Fall 2023), pp. 4–23.

Bílý, Matěj. *Varšavská smlouva 1969–1985: Vrchol a cesta k zániku* (Prague: Ústav pro studium totalitních režimů, 2016).

Bílý, Matěj. *Varšavská smlouva 1985–1991: Dezintegrace a rozpad* (Prague: Ústav pro studium totalitních režimů, 2021).

Bluth, Christoph. "The Warsaw Pact and Military Security in Central Europe during the Cold War," *Journal of Slavic Military Studies*, Vol. 17, No. 2 (April 2004), pp. 299–331.

Broadhurst, Arlene Idol, ed. *The Future of European Alliance Systems: NATO and the Warsaw Pact* (Boulder, CO: Westview Press, 1982).

Brown, Archie. *The Human Factor: Gorbachev, Reagan, and Thatcher, and the End of the Cold War* (New York: Oxford University Press, 2020).

Chernyaev, A. S., ed. *V Politbyuro TsK KPSS: Po zapisyam Anatoliya Chernyaeva, Vadima Medvedeva, Georgiya Shakhnazarova* (Moscow: Al'pina Biznes-Buks, 2006).

Chernyaev, A. S. *Shest' let s Gorbachevym: Po dnevnikovym zapisyam* (Moscow: Progress-Kul'tura, 1993).

Chernyaev, A. S., and A. B. Veber, eds. *Otvechaya na vyzov vremeni: Vneshnya politika perestroiki – Dokumental'nye svidetel'stva* (Moscow: Ves' mir, 2010).

Clawson, Robert W., and Lawrence S. Kaplan, eds. *The Warsaw Pact: Political Purpose and Military Means* (Wilmington, DE: Scholarly Resources, 1982).

Coker, Christopher. *NATO, the Warsaw Pact, and Africa* (Basingstoke: Macmillan, 1985).

Crow, Suzanne. "Negotiating New Treaties with Eastern Europe," *Radio Liberty Report on the USSR*, Vol. 2, No. 28 (July 19, 1991), pp. 3–6.

Crump, Laurien. *The Warsaw Pact Reconsidered: International Relations in Eastern Europe, 1955–69* (New York: Routledge, 2015).

Dashichev, Vyacheslav. "Vostok-zapad: poisk novykh otnoshenii – O prioritetakh vneshnei politiki Sovetskogo gosudarstva," *Literaturnaya gazeta* (Moscow), No. 20 (May 18, 1988), p. 14.

Dawisha, Karen, and Philip Hanson, eds. *Soviet-East European Dilemmas: Coercion, Competition, and Consent* (London: Holmes & Meier, 1981).

"De la Varşovia," *Scînteia* (Bucharest), August 20, 1989, p. 1.

"Deutschland, das neue Europa, und die Perestroika: Exklusivinterview mit Marschall Achromejev," *Neues Deutschland* (Berlin), October 4, 1990, p. 8.

Diedrich, Torsten, Winfried Heinemann, and Christian F. Ostermann, eds. *Der Warschauer Pakt: Von der Gründung bis zum Zusammenbruch 1955 bis 1991* (Berlin: Ch. Links Verlag, 2009).

"Dlya armii etot god budet perelomnym," *Krasnaya zvezda* (Moscow), April 17, 1991, p. 2.

"Dogovor ob okonchatel'nom uregulirovanii v otnoshenii Germanii," *Izvestiya* (Moscow), September 13, 1990, p. 4.

"Doklad General'nogo sekretarya TsK KPSS M. S. Gorbacheva na XIX Vsesoyuznoi konferentsii KPSS 28 iyunya 1988 goda," *Pravda* (Moscow), June 29, 1988, p. 3.

"Dokumenty: Polska-Rumunia," *Gazeta Wyborcza* (Warsaw), September 29 – October 1, 1989, p. 6.

"East-West Relations and Eastern Europe: The Soviet Perspective," *Problems of Communism*, Vol. 37, No. 3 (May–August 1988), pp. 60–67.

Easterly, William and Stanley Fischer. "The Soviet Economic Decline," *The World Bank Economic Review*, Vol. 9, No. 3 (September 1995), pp. 341–371.

Eyal, Jonathan, ed. *The Warsaw Pact and the Balkans: Moscow's Southern Flank* (Basingstoke: Macmillan, 1989).

Faringdon, Hugh. *Confrontation: The Strategic Geography of NATO and the Warsaw Pact* (London: Routledge, 1986).

Galkin, Aleksandr, and Anatolii Chernyaev, eds. *Mikhail Gorbachev i germanskii vopros: Sbornik dokumentov, 1986–1991* (Moscow: Ves' mir, 2006).

Gati, Charles. *Hungary and the Soviet Bloc* (Durham, NC: Duke University Press, 1986).

"Gomułka o inwazji na Czechoslowacje w sierpniu '68: Mysmy ich zaskoczyli akcja wojskowa," *Polityka* (Warsaw), No. 35 (August 29, 1992), p. 13.

Gorbachev, Mikhail. *Perestroika: New Thinking for Our Country and the World* (New York: Harper and Row, 1987).

Gorbachev, M. S. *Gody trudnykh reshenii* (Moscow: Al'fa-print, 1993).

Gribkov, A. I. *Sud'ba Varshavskogo Dogovora: Vospominaniya, dokumenty, fakty* (Moscow: Russkaya kniga, 1998), pp. 198–200.

Harrison, Mark. "Secrets, Lies, and Half Truths: The Decision to Disclose Soviet Defense Outlays," PERSA Working Paper No. 55 (Warwick: Political Economy Research in Soviet Archives, September 2008).

Harrison, Mark. "How Much Did the Soviets Really Spend on Defence? New Evidence from the Close of the Brezhnev Era," Warwick Economic Research Papers No. 662 (United Kingdom: University of Warwick, January 2003).

Henzler, Marek, and Włodzimierz Kalski. "Wyechali: Armia Radziecka z nami od dziecka," *Polityka* (Warsaw), No. 39 (September 25, 1993), pp. 12–13.

Heuser, Beatrice. "Warsaw Pact Military Doctrines in the 1970s and 1980s: Findings in the East German Archives," *Comparative Strategy*, Vol. 12, No. 4 (October–December 1993), pp. 437–457.

Hoffenaar, Jan, and Christopher Findlay, eds. *Military Planning for European Theatre Conflict in the Cold War: An Oral History Roundtable* (Zurich: Center for Security Studies, ETH-Zurich, 2007).

Holden, Gerald. *The Warsaw Pact: Soviet Security and Bloc Politics* (Oxford: Blackwell Books, 1989).

Holloway, David, and Jane M. O. Sharp, eds. *The Warsaw Pact: Alliance in Transition?* (Ithaca, NY: Cornell University Press, 1984).

Johnson, A. Ross, Robert W. Dean, and Alexander Alexiev. *East European Military Establishments: The Warsaw Pact Northern Tier* (New York: Crane, Russak, 1981).

Jones, Christopher D. *Soviet Influence in Eastern Europe: Political Autonomy and the Warsaw Pact* (New York: Pergamon, 1981).

Kanet, Roger E., ed. *The Soviet Union, Eastern Europe, and the Third World* (New York: Cambridge University Press, 1988).

Kanet, Roger E. "Military Relations between Eastern Europe and Africa," in Bruce E. Arlinghaus, ed., *Arms for Africa: Military Assistance and Foreign Policy in the Developing World* (Lexington, MA: Lexington Books, 1982), pp. 79–99.

Karner, Stefan, Mark Kramer, Peter Ruggenthaler, and Manfred Wilke, eds. *Der Kreml und die deutsche Wiedervereinigung 1990: Interne sowjetische Analysen* (Berlin: Metropol, 2015).

Karner, Stefan, Mark Kramer, Peter Ruggenthaler, and Manfred Wilke, eds., *Der Kreml und die Wende 1989: Interne Analysen der sowjetischen Führung zum Fall der kommunistischen Regime – Dokumente* (Innsbruck: Studien Verlag, 2014).

"Keleti ezredes a katonai szerződésrűl," *Népszabadság* (Budapest), June 14, 1991, p. 5.

Keßler, Heinz. *Zur Sache und zur Person: Erinnerungen* (Berlin: Edition Ost, 1996).

"Két hatalom közé ékelűdve: Interjú a lengyel külügyminiszterrel," *Népszabadság* (Budapest), June 6, 1991, pp. 1, 6.

King, Jeremy. "The Partial Soviet Troop Withdrawal from Hungary," RAD Background Report 166 (Munich: Radio Free Europe Research, September 11, 1989), p. 4.

Kolodziej, Edward A., and Roger E. Kanet, eds. *The Limits of Soviet Power in the Developing World* (Baltimore, MD: Johns Hopkins University Press, 1989).

"Kommyunike o vstreche vysshikh partiinykh i gosudarstvennykh deyatelei stran-uchastnits Varshavskogo Dogovora," *Krasnaya zvezda* (Moscow), April 27, 1985, pp. 1–2.

Korbonski, Andrzej, and Francis Fukuyama, eds. *The Soviet Union and the Third World: The Last Three Decades* (Ithaca, NY: Cornell University Press, 1987).

Kotkin, Stephen. *Armageddon Averted: The Soviet Collapse, 1970–2000*, updated ed. (New York: Oxford University Press, 2008).

Kovalev, S. "Suverenitet i internatsional'nye obyazannosti sotsialisticheskikh stran," *Pravda* (Moscow), September 26, 1968, p. 4.

Kozhokin, Mikhail. "Kreml' ozhidaet mnogogo ot byvshikh soyuznikov," *Moskovskie novosti* (Moscow), No. 22 (June 2, 1991), p. 3.

Kramer, Mark. "The Dissolution of the Soviet Union: A Case Study in Discontinuous Change," *Journal of Cold War Studies*, Vol. 24, No. 1 (Winter 2021–2022), pp. 188–218.

Kramer, Mark. "The USSR and Cold War Neutrality and Nonalignment in Europe," in Mark Kramer, Aryo Makko, and Peter Ruggenthaler, eds., *The Soviet Union and Cold War Neutrality and Nonalignment in Europe* (Lanham, MD: Rowman & Littlefield, 2021), pp. 533–565.

Kramer, Mark. "The Demise of the Soviet Bloc," *Journal of Modern History*, Vol. 83, No. 4 (December 2011), pp. 788–854.

Kramer, Mark. "The Kremlin, the Prague Spring, and the Brezhnev Doctrine," in Vladimir Tismaneanu, ed., *Promises of 1968: Crisis, Illusion, and Utopia* (Budapest: Central European University Press, 2011), pp. 251–252.

Kramer, Mark. "The Soviet Union, the Warsaw Pact, and the Polish Crisis of 1980–1981," in Lee Trepanier, Spasimir Domaradzki, and Jaclyn Stanke, eds., *The Solidarity Movement and Perspectives on the Last Decade of the Cold War* (Kraków: Oficyna Wydawoicza, 2010), pp. 27–67.

Kramer, Mark. *The Kukliński Files and the Polish Crisis of 1980–1981: An Analysis of the Newly Released Documents on Ryszard Kukliński*, CWIHP Working Paper No. 59 (Washington, DC: Cold War International History Project, March 2009).

Kramer, Mark. "Die Sowjetunion, der Warschauer Pakt und blockinterne Krisen während der Brežnev-Ära," in Torsten Diedrich, Winfried Heinemann, and Christian Ostermann, eds., *Der Warschauer Pakt: Von der Gründung bis zum Zusammenbruch 1955–1991* (Berlin: Ch. Links, 2008), pp. 273–337.

Kramer, Mark. "The Collapse of East European Communism and the Repercussions within the Soviet Union (Part 3)," *Journal of Cold War Studies*, Vol. 7, No. 1 (Winter 2004–2005), pp. 3–96.

Kramer, Mark. "The Collapse of East European Communism and the Repercussions within the Soviet Union (Part 2)," *Journal of Cold War Studies*, Vol. 6, No. 4 (Fall 2004), pp. 3–64.

Kramer, Mark. "The Collapse of East European Communism and the Repercussions within the Soviet Union (Part 1)," *Journal of Cold War Studies*, Vol. 5, No. 4 (Fall 2003), pp. 178–256.

Kramer, Mark. *Soviet Deliberations during the Polish Crisis, 1980–1981*, CWIHP Special Working Paper No. 1 (Washington, DC: Cold War International History Project, 1999).

Kramer, Mark. "'In Case Military Assistance Is Provided to Poland': Soviet Preparations for Military Contingencies, August 1980," *Cold War International History Project Bulletin*, No. 11 (Winter 1998), pp. 102–109.

Kramer, Mark. "Colonel Kukliński and the Polish Crisis," *Cold War International History Project Bulletin*, No. 11 (Winter 1998), pp. 48–59.

Kramer, Mark. "Jaruzelski, the Soviet Union, and the Imposition of Martial Law in Poland: New Light on the Mystery of December 1981," *Cold War International History Project Bulletin*, No. 11 (Winter 1998), pp. 5–32.

Kramer, Mark. "The Soviet Union and the 1956 Crises in Hungary and Poland: Reassessments and New Findings," *Journal of Contemporary History*, Vol. 33, No. 2 (April 1998), pp. 163–214.

Kramer, Mark. "NATO, Russia, and East European Security," in Uri Ra'anan and Kate Martin, eds., *Russia: A Return to Imperialism?* (New York: St. Martin's Press, 1995), pp. 105–160.

Kramer, Mark. "Warsaw Pact Military Planning in Central Europe: Revelations from the East German Archives," *Cold War International History Project Bulletin*, No. 2 (Fall 1992), pp. 1, 13–19.

Kramer, Mark. "The Role of the CPSU International Department in Soviet Foreign Relations and National Security Policy," *Soviet Studies*, Vol. 42, No. 2 (July 1990), pp. 429–447.

Kramer, Mark. "Air Defense Forces," in David R. Jones, ed., *Soviet Armed Forces Review Annual 1987–88* (Gulf Breeze, FL: Academic International Press, 1989), pp. 105–162.

Kramer, Mark. "Civil-Military Relations in the Warsaw Pact: The East European Component," *International Affairs*, Vol. 61, No. 1 (Winter 1985), pp. 45–67.

Kramer, Mark, and Vít Smetana, eds. *Imposing, Maintaining, and Tearing Open the Iron Curtain: The Cold War and East-Central Europe, 1945–1990* (Lanham, MD: Rowman & Littlefield, 2013).

Krenz, Egon. *Herbst '89* (Berlin: Neues Leben, 1999).

Krenz, Egon. *Wenn Mauern fallen: Die friedliche Revolution – Vorgeschichte, Ablauf-Auswirkungen* (Vienna: Paul Neff, 1990).

Labetskaya, Ekaterina. "Marshal Kulikov: 'Voennye byli slishkom poslushnymi'," *Vremya MN* (Moscow), September 6, 1999, p. 2.

"Lépés egy összeurópai biztonsági rendszer felé," *Népszabadság* (Budapest), February 26, 1991, p. 6.

Luk'yanov, Fedor. "My ne khotim byt' neitral'nymi, zayavil vengerskii prem'er," *Izvestiya* (Moscow), May 1, 1991, p. 4.

Mack, Hans-Hubertus, László Veszprémy, and Rüdiger Wenzke. *Die NVA und die Ungarische Volksarmee im Warschauer Pakt* (Potsdam: Militärgeschichtliches Forschungsamt, 2019).

"Magyar-szovjet tárgyalások: Időrekord helyett jó szerződést," *Népszabadság* (Budapest), April 29, 1991, pp. 1, 3.

Maslanka, Susanne. "The Withdrawal of the GDR from the Warsaw Pact: Expectations, Hopes, and Disappointments in German-Soviet Relations during the Dissociation Process," *Historical Social Research*, Vol. 47, No. 2 (2022), pp. 53–76.

Mastny, Vojtech, and Malcolm Byrne, eds. *A Cardboard Castle? An Inside History of the Warsaw Pact, 1955–1991* (Budapest: Central European University Press, 2005).

Mastny, Vojtech, Sven Holtsmark, and Andreas Wenger, eds. *War Plans and Alliances in the Cold War: Threat Perceptions in the East and West* (New York: Routledge, 2006).

Matějka, Zdeněk. "How the Warsaw Pact Was Dissolved," *Perspectives*, No. 8 (Summer 1997), pp. 55–65.

Matlock Jr., Jack F. *Autopsy on an Empire: The American Ambassador's Account of the Collapse of the Soviet Union* (New York: Random House, 1995), pp. 190–192.

Medvedev, Vadim. *Raspad: Kak on nazreval v "mirovoi sisteme sotsializma"* (Moscow: Mezhdunarodnye otnosheniya, 1994).

Miles, Simon. "We All Fall Down: The Dismantling of the Warsaw Pact and the End of the Cold War in Eastern Europe," *International Security*, Vol. 48, No. 3 (Winter 2023/24), pp. 51–85.

"Ministr inostrannykh del SSSR ob uprazdnenii Varshavskogo Dogovora i ego posledstviyakh dlya Evropy, SSSR, i polozhenii v Yugoslavii," *Izvestiya* (Moscow), July 4, 1991, p. 2.

"Miting Chekhoslovatsko-sovetskoi druzhby: Rech' tovarishcha Gorbacheva M. S.," *Pravda* (Moscow), April 11, 1987, p. 2.

Modrow, Hans. *In historischer Mission: als deutscher Politiker unterwegs* (Berlin: Edition Ost, 2007).

Modrow, Hans. *Aufbruch und Ende* (Hamburg: Konkret Literatur, 1991).

Muehlenbeck, Philip E., and Natalia Telepneva, eds. *Warsaw Pact Intervention in the Third World: Aid and Influence in the Cold War* (London: I.B. Tauris, 2018).

"Na nachalakh razumnoi i nadezhnoi dostatochnosti dlya oborony," *Krasnaya zvezda* (Moscow), April 4, 1991, p. 2.

"NATO: A Szovjetunió beléphet," *Magyar Hirlap* (Budapest), February 28, 1991, p. 3.

"Ne nado dramatizirovat," *Izvestiya* (Moscow), May 7, 1991, p. 3.

Nelson, Daniel N., ed. *Soviet Allies: The Warsaw Pact and the Issue of Reliability* (Boulder, CO: Westview Press, 1984).

"Nyama predvaritelni usloviya za razgovorite mezhdu Popov i Pavlov," *Otechestven vestnik* (Sofia), May 16, 1991, pp. 1–2.

"O razvitii obstanovki v Vostochnoi Evrope i nashei politike v etom regione: Postanovlenie Sekretariata TsK Kommunisticheskoi Partii Sovetskogo Soyuza," *Izvestiya TsK KPSS* (Moscow), No. 3 (March 1991), pp. 12–17.

"O sozyve ocherednogo XXVII S"ezda KPSS i zadachakh svyazannykh s ego podgotovkoi i provedeniem: Doklad General'nogo sekretarya TsK KPSS M. S. Gorbacheva," *Pravda* (Moscow), April 23, 1985, p. 2.

"O voennoi doktrine gosudarstv-uchastnikov Varshavskogo Dogovora," *Krasnaya zvezda* (Moscow), May 30, 1987, p. 1.

"Obshchie tseli, edinyi kurs: Prebyvanie M. S. Gorbacheva v Slovakii," *Pravda* (Moscow), April 12, 1987, p. 1.

Odom, William E. *The Collapse of the Soviet Military* (New Haven, CT: Yale University Press, 1998).

"Oktyabr' i perestroika: Revolyutsiya prodolzhaetsya – Doklad General'nogo sekretarya TsK KPSS M. S. Gorbacheva," *Pravda* (Moscow), November 3, 1987, p. 5.

Plokhy, Serhii. *The Last Empire: The Final Days of the Soviet Union* (New York: Basic Books, 2014).

"Pobeda: Pamyat' i pobeda," *Pravda* (Moscow), May 9, 1991, p. 3.

"Podpisanie dogovora o druzhbe, sotrudnichestve i vzaimnoi pomoshchi," *Pravda* (Moscow), May 15, 1955, p. 1.

"Podpishet li Bolgariya dogovor?" *Izvestiya* (Moscow), May 1, 1991, p. 1.

Pokholenchuk, Colonel B., and Lieutenant-Colonel V. Gavrilenko. "Po zakonam vysokoi otvetsvennosti: Sobraniya partiinogo aktiva Moskovskogo okruga PVO," *Krasnaya zvezda* (Moscow), June 17, 1987, p. 2.

"Programma Kommunisticheskoi partii Sovetskogo Soyuza," *Pravda* (Moscow), March 7, 1986, p. 7.

"Protokol o prekrashchenii deistviya Dogovora o druzhbe, sotrudnichestve i vzaimnoi pomoshchi, podpisannogo v Varshave 14 maya 1955 goda, i Protokola o prodlenii sroka ego deistviya, podpisannogo 26 aprelya 1985 goda v Varshave," *Izvestiya* (Moscow), July 3, 1991, p. 5.

"Rech' General'nogo sekretarya TsK KPSS tovarishcha M.S. Gorbacheva na Plenume TsK KPSS 11 marta 1985 goda," *Pravda* (Moscow), March 12, 1985, p. 3.

"Rech' M. S. Gorbacheva," *Izvestiya* (Moscow), July 7, 1989, p. 2.

"Rech' M. S. Gorbacheva na vstreche s trudyashchimisya v g. Kieve," *Krasnaya zvezda* (Moscow), February 24, 1989, p. 3.

Reisch, Alfred. "Hungary: The Hard Task of Setting Relations with the USSR on a New Footing," *Radio Free Europe Report on Eastern Europe*, Vol. 2, No. 20 (May 24, 1991), pp. 15–19.

Rodionov, B. "Nakhodit' vzaimopriemlemye formuly: Kakimi budut dogovory SSSR s sosedyami v Vostochnoi Evrope," *Izvestiya* (Moscow), June 4, 1991, p. 5.

Sadykiewicz, Michael. *The Warsaw Pact Command Structure in Peace and War*, RAND Report No. R-3558-RC (Santa Monica, CA: RAND Corporation, September 1988).

Saunders, Chris, Helder Adegar Fonseca, and Lena Dallywater, eds. *Eastern Europe, the Soviet Union, and Africa: New Perspectives on the Era of Decolonization, 1950s to 1990s* (Oldenbourg: De Gruyter, 2023).

Scurtu, Ioan, ed. *România: Retragerea trupelor sovietice. 1958* (Bucharest: Didactică și Pedagogică, 1996).

Shtemenko, Army-General S. M. "Bratstvo rozhdennoe v boyu," *Za rubezhom* (Moscow), No. 19 (May 1976), p. 7.

Simon, Jeffrey. *Warsaw Pact Forces: Problems of Command and Control* (Boulder, CO: Westview Press, 1985).

"Sluzhu Sovetskomu Soyuzu!" *Pravda* (Moscow), February 23, 1991, pp. 1–2.

Socor, Vladimir. "The Romanian-Soviet Friendship Treaty and Its Regional Implications," *Radio Free Europe Report on Eastern Europe*, Vol. 2, No. 17 (May 3, 1991), pp. 25–33.

"Sovetsko-yugoslavskaya deklaratsiya," *Pravda* (Moscow), March 19, 1988, p. 1.

Storkmann, Klaus. "East Germany as Player in the 'Global Cold War'? East Germany's Military Commitment to Africa and the Middle East, and Its Coordination with the Soviet Leadership," *Revista de istorie militară* (Bucharest), No. 3 (2019), pp. 111–125.

Storkmann, Klaus. "East German Military Aid to the Sandinista Government of Nicaragua, 1979–1990," *Journal of Cold War Studies*, Vol. 16, No. 2 (Spring 2014), pp. 56–76.

Storkmann, Klaus. *Geheime Solidarität: Militärbeziehungen und Militärhilfen der DDR in die Dritte Welt* (Berlin: Christoph Links Verlag, 2012).

Stourzh, Gerald, and Wolfgang Mueller. *A Cold War over Austria: The Struggle for the State Treaty, Neutrality, and the End of East-West Occupation, 1945–1955* (Lanham, MD: Lexington Books, 2018).

"Strakh pered morozom," *Izvestiya* (Moscow), March 17, 1987, p. 3.

Suppan, Arnold, Gerald Stourzh, and Wolfgang Mueller, eds. *Der österreichische Staatsvertrag* (Vienna: Böhlau, 2005).

Taylor, Brian D. "The Soviet Military and the Disintegration of the USSR," *Journal of Cold War Studies*, Vol. 5, No. 1 (Winter 2003), pp. 17–66.

Terry, Sarah Meiklejohn, ed. *Soviet Policy in Eastern Europe* (New Haven, CT: Yale University Press, 1984).

"Tratat de colaborare, bună vecinătate, şi amiciţie între România Uniunea Republicilor Sovietice Socialiste," *România Liberă* (Bucharest), April 12, 1991, p. 8.

"U nas svoya chest'," *Sovetskaya Rossiya* (Moscow), February 23, 1991, pp. 1–2.

"Ugrás a sötétbe: Vállalatvezetűk a szovjet kapcsolatról," *Beszélő* (Budapest), May 25, 1991, p. 9.

Umbach, Frank. *Das rote Bündnis: Entwicklung und Zerfall des Warschauer Pakts 1955–1991* (Berlin: Ch. Links Verlag, 2005).

U.S. Central Intelligence Agency, Center for the Study of Intelligence. *At Cold War's End: U.S. Intelligence on the Soviet Union and Eastern Europe, 1989–1991* (Washington, DC: CIA 1999).

U.S. Central Intelligence Agency, Historical Review Program. *Warsaw Pact Wartime Statutes: Instruments of Control* (Washington, DC: U.S. Government Printing Office, 2011).

U.S. Central Intelligence (CIA). "The Warsaw Pact: Its Role in Soviet Bloc Affairs from Its Origin to the Present Day," Intelligence Analytical Report, May 6, 1966, released September 2002.

Vladimirov, O (pseud.). "Vedushchii faktor mirovogo revolyutsionnogo protsessa," *Pravda* (Moscow), June 21, 1985, pp. 3–4.

Völgyes, Iván. *The Political Reliability of the Warsaw Pact Armies: The Southern Tier* (Durham, NC: Duke University Press, 1982).

"Vystuplenie M. S. Gorbacheva v Organizatsii Ob"edinennykh Natsii," *Pravda* (Moscow), December 8, 1988, p. 2.

Wenger, Andreas, Vojtech Mastny, and Christian Nuenlist, eds. *Origins of the European Security System: The Helsinki Process Revisited 1965–75* (New York: Routledge, 2008).

Wenzke, Rüdiger, ed. *Die Streitkräfte der DDR und Polens in der Operationsplanung des Warschauer Paktes* (Potsdam: Militärgeschichtliches Forschungsamt, 2010).

Wenzke, Rüdiger, *Die NVA und der Prager Frühling 1968: Die Rolle Ulbrichts under der DDR-Streitkräfte bei der Niederschlagung der tschechoslowakischen Reformbewegung* (Berlin: Links Verlag, 1995).

Wenzke, Rüdiger, *Prager Frühling – Prager Herbst: Zur Intervention der Warschauer-Pakt-Streitkräfte in der ČSSR 1968, Fakten und Zusammenhange* (Berlin: Dunckere Humblot, 1990).

Wettig, Gerhard. *Gorbatschow: Reformpolitik und Warschauer Pakt, 1985–1991* (Innsbruck: Studien Verlag, 2021).

Wolfe, Thomas W. *Soviet Power and Europe, 1945–1970* (Baltimore, MD: Johns Hopkins University Press, 1970).

Woycicki, Kazimierz. "Szansa dla Europy Środkowej: Zbliżenie polsko-czechosłowacko-węgierskie," *Życie Warszawy* (Warsaw), January 22, 1991, pp. 1, 4.

"X Zjazd Polskiej Zjednoczonej Partii Robotniczej – wystąpienie tow. Gorbaczowa M. S.," *Trybuna Ludu* (Warsaw), July 1, 1986, p. 1.

Yazov, Dmitrii. *Udary sud'by: Vospominaniya soldata i marshala* (Moscow: Kniga i biznes, 2002), pp. 359–360.

"Zashchita sotsializma – vysshii internatsional'nyi dolg," *Pravda* (Moscow), August 22, 1968, pp. 2–3.

"Zayavlenie prezidenta ChSFR," *Izvestiya* (Moscow), April 30, 1991, p. 1.

"Zayavlenie rukovoditelei Bolgarii, Vengrii, GDR, Pol'shi, i Sovetskogo Soyuza," *Izvestiya* (Moscow), December 5, 1989, p. 2.

"Zayavlenie Sovetskogo pravitel'stva," *Izvestiya* (Moscow), December 5, 1989, p. 2.

Zheglov, Major M. "Varshavskii Dogovor i evropeiskaya bezopasnost'," *Krasnaya zvezda* (Moscow), February 22, 1991, p. 3.

Zubok, Vladislav M. *Collapse: The Fall of the Soviet Union* (New Haven, CT: Yale University Press, 2021).

Cambridge Elements

Soviet and Post-Soviet History

Mark Edele
University of Melbourne

Mark Edele teaches Soviet history at the University of Melbourne, where he is Hansen Professor in History. His most recent books are *Stalinism at War* (2021) and *Russia's War Against Ukraine* (2023). He is one of the convenors of the Research Initiative on Post-Soviet Space (RIPSS) at the University of Melbourne.

Rebecca Friedman
Florida International University

Rebecca Friedman is Founding Director of the Wolfsonian Public Humanities Lab and Professor of History at Florida International University in Miami. Her recent book, Modernity, Domesticity and Temporality: Time at Home, supported by the National Endowment for the Humanities, explores modern time and home in twentieth century Russia (2020). She is one of the editors for the Bloomsbury Academic series A Cultural History of Time.

About the Series

Elements in Soviet and Post-Soviet History pluralise the history of the former Soviet space. Contributions decolonise Soviet history and provincialise the former metropole: Russia. In doing so, the series provides an up-to-date history of the present of the region formerly known as the Soviet Union.

Cambridge Elements

Soviet and Post-Soviet History

Elements in the Series

Making National Diasporas: Soviet-Era Migrations and Post-Soviet Consequences
Lewis H. Siegelbaum and Leslie Page Moch

Ukraine not 'the' Ukraine
Marta Dyczok

The Fate of the Soviet Bloc's Military Alliance: Reform, Adaptation, and Collapse of the Warsaw Pact, 1985–1991
Mark Kramer

A full series listing is available at: www.cambridge.org/ESPH

For EU product safety concerns, contact us at Calle de José Abascal, 56–1°,
28003 Madrid, Spain or eugpsr@cambridge.org.

www.ingramcontent.com/pod-product-compliance
Lightning Source LLC
LaVergne TN
LVHW020352260326
834688LV00045B/1675